Python® For Kids

FOR DUMMIES®

A Wiley Brand

by Brendan Scott

FOR DUMMIES®
A Wiley Brand

Python® For Kids For Dummies®

Published by: **John Wiley & Sons, Inc.,** 111 River Street, Hoboken, NJ 07030-5774, www.wiley.com

Copyright © 2015 by John Wiley & Sons, Inc., Hoboken, New Jersey

Media and software compilation copyright © 2015 by John Wiley & Sons, Inc. All rights reserved.

Published simultaneously in Canada

No part of this publication may be reproduced, stored in a retrieval system or transmitted in any form or by any means, electronic, mechanical, photocopying, recording, scanning or otherwise, except as permitted under Sections 107 or 108 of the 1976 United States Copyright Act, without the prior written permission of the Publisher. Requests to the Publisher for permission should be addressed to the Permissions Department, John Wiley & Sons, Inc., 111 River Street, Hoboken, NJ 07030, (201) 748-6011, fax (201) 748-6008, or online at http://www.wiley.com/go/permissions.

Trademarks: Wiley, For Dummies, the Dummies Man logo, Dummies.com, Making Everything Easier, and related trade dress are trademarks or registered trademarks of John Wiley & Sons, Inc. and may not be used without written permission. Python is a registered trademark of Python Software Foundation. All other trademarks are the property of their respective owners. John Wiley & Sons, Inc. is not associated with any product or vendor mentioned in this book.

LIMIT OF LIABILITY/DISCLAIMER OF WARRANTY: THE PUBLISHER AND THE AUTHOR MAKE NO REPRESENTATIONS OR WARRANTIES WITH RESPECT TO THE ACCURACY OR COMPLETENESS OF THE CONTENTS OF THIS WORK AND SPECIFICALLY DISCLAIM ALL WARRANTIES, INCLUDING WITHOUT LIMITATION WARRANTIES OF FITNESS FOR A PARTICULAR PURPOSE. NO WARRANTY MAY BE CREATED OR EXTENDED BY SALES OR PROMOTIONAL MATERIALS. THE ADVICE AND STRATEGIES CONTAINED HEREIN MAY NOT BE SUITABLE FOR EVERY SITUATION. THIS WORK IS SOLD WITH THE UNDERSTANDING THAT THE PUBLISHER IS NOT ENGAGED IN RENDERING LEGAL, ACCOUNTING, OR OTHER PROFESSIONAL SERVICES. IF PROFESSIONAL ASSISTANCE IS REQUIRED, THE SERVICES OF A COMPETENT PROFESSIONAL PERSON SHOULD BE SOUGHT. NEITHER THE PUBLISHER NOR THE AUTHOR SHALL BE LIABLE FOR DAMAGES ARISING HEREFROM. THE FACT THAT AN ORGANIZATION OR WEBSITE IS REFERRED TO IN THIS WORK AS A CITATION AND/OR A POTENTIAL SOURCE OF FURTHER INFORMATION DOES NOT MEAN THAT THE AUTHOR OR THE PUBLISHER ENDORSES THE INFORMATION THE ORGANIZATION OR WEBSITE MAY PROVIDE OR RECOMMENDATIONS IT MAY MAKE. FURTHER, READERS SHOULD BE AWARE THAT INTERNET WEBSITES LISTED IN THIS WORK MAY HAVE CHANGED OR DISAPPEARED BETWEEN WHEN THIS WORK WAS WRITTEN AND WHEN IT IS READ.

For general information on our other products and services, please contact our Customer Care Department within the U.S. at 877-762-2974, outside the U.S. at 317-572-3993, or fax 317-572-4002. For technical support, please visit www.wiley.com/techsupport.

Wiley publishes in a variety of print and electronic formats and by print-on-demand. Some material included with standard print versions of this book may not be included in e-books or in print-on-demand. If this book refers to media such as a CD or DVD that is not included in the version you purchased, you may download this material at http://booksupport.wiley.com. For more information about Wiley products, visit www.wiley.com.

Library of Congress Control Number: 2015944529

ISBN 978-1-119-09310-7 (pbk); ISBN 978-1-119-11216-7 (ebk); ISBN 978-1-119-11085-9 (ebk)

Manufactured in the United States of America

10 9 8 7 6 5 4 3 2

Contents

Introduction

Hi! Welcome to the book. You're going on a tour of all things Python. If you join me and code along with the projects, you'll have your basic Python programming wings by the end of the book.

Everything in this book you need to know by *doing* — typing in the code or, better yet, thinking up the code before reading what I've done.

About This Book

This book walks you through all the parts you have to know about Python programming. You get examples. I talk about planning programs. And I help link you with the broader Python community so that you can head out there after mastering the projects in this book.

Conventions Used

Keep these things in mind while you read:

- Sometimes words are in *italics* and then I explain the words. Here is an example: "The objects in the list are called *elements*." When you see this sentence, you know to keep your eyes peeled for a definition. (Elements are the objects in a list.)

- Python code is written in a different font from the other text. Sometimes it's inline with the text and looks like this: `print('Hello World!')`.

✒ Sometimes it's a separate block of text, like this:

```
print('Hello World!')
```

✒ Some code blocks have a >>> at the front of some lines. I'm showing you what happens when you're using an interactive Python prompt. You need to type the code that follows the >>> in this book into the Python console that's running on your computer to see what happens:

```
>>> my_message = "Hello World!"
>>> print(my_message)
```

✒ The number of spaces at the front of each line of code is important. The length of your lines isn't (technically) significant, but Python style guidelines suggest lines with no more than 79 *characters* (letters, numbers, spaces, or punctuation marks). This book isn't as wide as your screen; it only lets me show 69 characters in a line. I've *broken* (split) some lines of code in the book. I split them to make sure that the code works and prints the right way. Be careful when you type them in! It's not always clear how many spaces are at the front of the broken line.

✒ I split lines two ways.

● The first is *implicitly.* Basically, you can split the code in between any pair of parentheses at a comma. Python still sees it as a single line. The second and later parts of a split line should be indented to where the parentheses opened. Here's an example from the code in Project 9:

```
values = (e.first_name, e.family_name,
          e.date_of_birth, e.email_address)
```

Even though you type this as two separate lines, Python sees it as a single line. (Think of it as one long line.) Type this code as you see it, pressing Enter at the end of each line and typing spaces at the start of each line so that the first character in the line is in the right place.

- The second way to split a line is *explicitly* with the backslash character: \ (not /). Here's an example from Project 9:

```
raw_input_prompt = "Press: 1 for training,"+\
                   " 2 for testing, 3 to quit.\n"
```

You type these as two separate lines, with the \ at the end of the first line. However, Python sees it as a single line.

↙ When using the Python interpreter in Projects 2 and 3 only, each new line starts with either . . . or >>>. If you don't see these in the code in the book, then the previous line is meant to be typed in as one long line. For example, the following code is from Project 2:

```
>>> my_second_message = 'This name is a little long.
    Ideally, try to keep the name short, but not too
    short.'
```

This code doesn't have . . . or >>> at the start of the second or third line. This means you're supposed to type it all in before pressing Enter. Only press Enter after typing too short.' at the end, *not* after typing little long. and but not.

↙ Sometimes the output on your computer may look a little different from what you see in this book. For example, when you run a program in later projects, you might see a restart line. On my screen, all the following text is on a single line:

```
>>> ================================= RESTART
==============================
```

↙ In Project 4 you see how to automatically indent your code. Until then, each time you need to indent code, do it by pressing the spacebar four times before you add your code. If you have to indent code two levels, press the spacebar eight times (that's two levels of indent by four spaces per level) before typing your code, and so on. You need to do this for each line of the indented code.

✔ When I'm explaining how code works, I often provide a *code template* — an outline of how to use the code. A sample template is: `help([object name])`. In this template, the keyword is `help`, and it needs to be followed by a pair of parentheses. The square brackets indicate something which is optional. The italics mean you need to fill in. Everything not in italics, type it just like it looks. Using this template, the code `help(help)` works (it gets help on the `help` keyword), and so does `help()`, with nothing inside the parentheses (since *[object name]* was optional).

✔ Web addresses (URLs) and programming code are in `monofont`. If you're reading this book on a device connected to the Internet, you can click the address to visit that website. Try it: `www.dummies.com`.

✔ Sometimes you need to choose something from a menu. I'm not talking about a burger and fries. I mean actions. For example, I might ask you to choose File ➪ New File. This means that you go to the File menu and choose New File from it.

✔ The word Ctrl means the Ctrl key on your keyboard. Ctrl+A means that you press the key marked Ctrl while you press the A key. All at the same time. Then release both keys. If you're using a Mac, your keyboard has a control key — use it. Ctrl-A means press the control key down and press the A key. Then release both keys. Don't use the option or command keys.

✔ If you're using a Mac, assume that when I say Enter key, it means the Return key on your keyboard.

Foolish Assumptions

I've tried not to make too many assumptions about you in this book. In order to use this book, you need to be able to turn on your computer and navigate the Start Menu (on Windows). To install Python you will need administrator access for the computer you're installing it on.

Learning anything is slow going to start. You are going to need a bit of determination to make it through the book. Hang in there.

Icons Used in This Book

The Warning icon tells you to watch out! This information may save you headaches. In some cases, you could lose data if you don't heed the warnings.

You're gonna use this information for a long, long time. Commit it to long-term gray matter.

The Tip icon marks shortcuts that make programming easier.

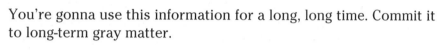

Coding Connections icons mark information that applies not just to Python, but to coding in general.

Beyond the Book

You can find a bunch more information outside this book. Check out:

✔ **Cheat Sheet:** This book has an online cheat sheet at www.dummies.com/cheatsheet/pythonforkids. The Cheat Sheet has a list of Python keywords, common built-ins, and selected functions from the standard library. Use it as a quick reference when you're coding.

✔ **Dummies.com online articles and bonus projects:** In addition to the projects in this book, there are some bonus projects online. You can get them from www.dummies.com/extras/pythonforkids.

✔ python4kids.brendanscott.com: Visit my Python for Kids blog. Many of the projects in this book started out there. The blog has a dedicated blog entry for each of the projects and has a heap of other things you can try, too. If you've got feedback, you can leave it on the blog page that applies.

Where to Go from Here

Right now you should go to Project 1 to read more about what this language can do and to install it. Before you move on to Project 2, make sure you know about Ctrl+C. Then you're ready to write your first Python program! Move in and out of the projects as you like. The code in each project stands on its own. Be careful though — even though they don't use *code* from earlier projects, they often use *concepts* introduced earlier.

Week 1
Slithering into Python

```
! Hello World! Hello World! Hello World! Hello World! Hello World! Hello World!
Hello World! Hello World! Hello World! Hello World! Hello World! Hello World!
llo World! Hello World! Hello World! Hello World! Hello World! Hello World! Hell
o World! Hello World! Hello World! Hello World! Hello World! Hello World! Hello
World! Hello World! Hello World! Hello World! Hello World! Hello World! Hello Wo
rld! Hello World! Hello World! Hello World! Hello World! Hello World! Hello Worl
d! Hello World! Hello World! Hello World! Hello World! Hello World! Hello World!
 Hello World! Hello World! Hello World! Hello World! Hello World! Hello World! H
ello World! Hello World! Hello World! Hello World! Hello World! Hello World! Hel
lo World! Hello World! Hello World! Hello World! Hello World! Hello World! Hello
 World! Hello World! Hello World! Hello World! Hello World! Hello World! Hello W
orld! Hello World! Hello World! Hello World! Hello World! Hello World! Hello Wor
ld! Hello World! Hello World! Hello World! Hello World! Hello World! Hello World
! Hello World! Hello World! Hello World! Hello World! Hello World! Hello World!
Hello World! Hello World! Hello World! Hello World! Hello World! Hello World! He
llo World! Hello World! Hello World! Hello World! Hello World! Hello World! Hell
o World! Hello World! Hello World! Hello World! Hello World! Hello World! Hello
World! Hello World! Hello World! Hello World! Hello World! Hello World! Hello Wo
rld! Hello World! Hello World! Hello World! Hello World! Hello World! Hello Worl
d! Hello World! Hello World! Hello World! Hello World! Hello World! Hello World!
 Hello World! Hello World! Hello World! Hello World! Hello World! Hello World! H
ello World! Hello World! Hello World! Hello World! Hello World! Hello World! Hel
lo World! Hello World! Hello World! Hello World! Hello World! Hello World! Hello
 World! Hello World! Hello World! Hello World! Hello World!
>>>
```

This week you're . . .

Getting Started with Python

In this project, you're introduced to Python: where it's used and what it's used for. I explain the two current versions of Python. This book is focused on Python 2.7 and I explain why. With my help during this chapter, you install a copy of Python 2.7 (if you don't already have it installed) and fire it up. I also tell you how to stop once you've started.

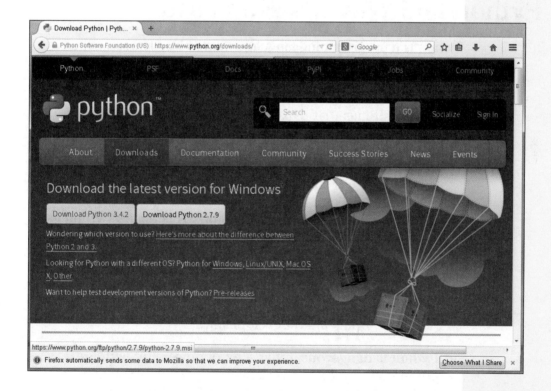

This project also shows you how to get Python's documentation, both built in to Python and online. I give you ways to search online for answers to your Python problems, just in case you've never searched the Internet before. You also read about the Python community, which is one place you can go for help or new ideas. All that, but no actual programming? No worries. Actual programming starts in Project 2.

TL;DR: If you've already installed Python, and you can start and stop it, then skip to Project 2.

Python and Why It's Wonderful

Python is a programming language written by a person called Guido van Rossum in the 1990s. *Programming* languages allow you to control what a computer does and the way it does it.

Some of the things that make Python totes awesome (also known as "really helpful and lots of fun") are:

- **Python code is easy to read and understand.** In fact, I think Python's code is sublime and beautiful. (Hey, that's just my opinion.) Its beauty means you don't even notice the way Python makes complex things simple. This makes Python easy to learn, which makes it perfect for kids.

- **Python is productive.** It makes tough tasks simple. Almost any programming task is easier with Python than it is with other programming languages. Computer types call this *RAD* (for Rapid Application Development).

- **Python is dangerous.** It has a lot of power. But with great power comes great responsibility. (Remember Spider-Man?) And you'll have to use your powers for good, not evil. (If you want to use them for evil, you have to stop reading now.)

- **Python is a scripting language.** The programs are fed into Python's interpreter, which runs them directly, so there's no compiling (which is the case for some other languages). It is faster and easier to get feedback on your Python code (finding errors, for example). Python means you complete and *execute* (run) your programs faster and that makes programming fun!

✔ **Python is cross platform.** Almost anyone can use it, no matter what computer operating system they have. You can run pretty much any Python program on Windows, Mac, and Linux personal computers and from large servers through to tiny computers like the Raspberry Pi. (A Pi-specific project is waiting at dummies.com/go/pythonforkids for you.) You can even run Python programs on Android and iOS tablets. I even used my Android tablet to code some of the early projects in this book.

✔ **Python uses dynamic typing for its variables.** This may not mean much to you if you've never done programming before. Dynamically typed variables make programming easier because they let you just start using a variable, rather than first explaining to the computer what the variable is supposed to be.

✔ **Python gets lots of help from *third-party modules*.** This means that a lot of other people (third parties) have written libraries. A *library* is a bunch of code for doing something specific. This makes your work easier because you don't have to start from scratch every time you write a new program; sometimes you can use the libraries already written. The Minecraft project online uses a third-party library to change a Minecraft game on a Raspberry Pi.

✔ **Python is free software.** This means that the license terms for Python respect your freedom. I think this is pretty important. You can download and run Python without paying any money, and any program that you write with it is yours to use and share any way you want. It also means that the Python *source code* (the human-readable form of what the computer runs) is available so, when you're feeling brave enough, you can look at how the Python developers wrote their code. (It's written in a different programming language, though, d'oh!)

Pythons aren't just snakes

The Python programming language is named after a comedy group called Monty Python, not the reptile. Monty Python was active mainly in the 1970s. (40 years ago! Forever and ever, right?) They had a British television show called *Monty Python's Flying Circus* and have made lots of movies, the most notable of which is *Monty Python and the Holy Grail*.

Who's Using Python

Python is used just about everywhere.

- ✔ **In space:** The International Space Station's Robonaut 2 robot uses Python for its central command system. Python is planned for use in a European mission to Mars in 2020 to collect soil samples.

- ✔ **In particle physics laboratories:** Python helps understand the data analysis from some atom smashing experiments at the CERN Large Hadron Collider.

- ✔ **In astronomy:** The MeerKat Radio telescope array (the largest radio telescope in the Southern Hemisphere) uses Python for its control and monitoring systems.

- ✔ **In movie studios:** Industrial Light and Magic (*Star Wars* geniuses) uses Python to automate its movie production processes. Side Effects Software's computer-generated imagery program Houdini uses Python for its programming interface and to script the engine.

- ✔ **In games:** Activision uses Python for building games, testing, and analyzing stuff. They even use Python to find people cheating by boosting each other.

✔ **In the music industry:** Spotify music streaming service uses Python to send you music.

✔ **In the video industry:** Netflix uses Python to make sure movies play *(stream)* without stopping. Python is used a lot for YouTube.

✔ **In Internet search:** Google used Python all over in its early development phase.

✔ **In medicine:** The Nodality company uses Python to handle information that they use to search for a cure to cancer.

✔ **In your OS (admin-ing your datas):** Operating systems like Linux and Mac OSX use Python for some of their administrative functions.

✔ **In your doorbell:** Rupa Dachere and Akkana Peck say that you can automate your home with Python, hooking up sensors to your house. With it you can, for example, open and close the curtains or automatically turn on lights when you come in the room.

I could go on. The point is that Python will apply to whatever you're interested in, no matter what it is.

Making Things with Python

You do these things while you work through this book:

✔ Make a math trainer for practicing your times tables.

✔ Make a simple *encryption* (a secret code) program.

✔ Use Python on a Raspberry Pi to work with and modify your Minecraft world. (See `www.dummies.com/go/pythonforkids` for that project.)

When you've honed your mad skills and are ready to move on, there'll be other things you can do:

- Using `Tkinter` (or other widget sets), you can write user applications that use graphics rather than just text to interact with the user.

- You can extend other programs like Blender (a 3D modeling program), GIMP (a 2D photo-retouching program), and LibreOffice (office programs), among many others by writing custom scripts. I had to fix some 3D models I was making in Blender. It would've taken forever to do by hand, so I wrote a Python script to do it quickly.

- You can write games with graphics using `Tkinter` or the Pygame or Kivy libraries. The games in this book are text only.

- You can use the matplotlib library to draw complex graphs for your math or science courses.

- Using the openCV library, you can experiment with computer vision. People who are into robotics use it to help their robots see and grab things and to avoid obstacles when moving.

Whatever you want it to do, there's a good chance someone has already written code to do it or to help you do it yourself.

Understanding This Book's Pedagogical Approach

That title is just to impress your parents. (I hope they're not reading this part. But look: If they don't see that title, tell them that this book *has* a pedagogical approach — *ped-uh-goj-i-cul*. It means education or teaching.)

The point of this book is to give you a chunk of information about the programming concepts that you need to program in Python. The book is for you — a kid who can learn Python.

I am thorough

Thorough, yes. Will I include everything? No way. Many aspects of Python have lots of options. If I took you through all the possibilities of each option, you'd fall asleep (or throw this book out the window). If you do either of those things, then you won't be learning.

As you read, remember that I've tried to introduce you to enough information so you can be a Python programmer, but not so much that you'd need superhuman powers to get through it. Expand on your own using the documentation and help.

You start pretty slowly with *core* (main) principles. If you think things aren't going fast enough, skip ahead! The examples are generally self contained. This means that you end up with many smaller projects rather than a few larger projects. I did that on purpose so you can do the projects in any order you like. You've got enough people telling you what to do. You can go where you want to in this book.

The earlier projects use plain English, rather than technical words. As you go through the book, you'll see more jargon. You'll also get less hand holding. You'll have to work harder the further you get through the book.

If you're dying to know more

If you really want to know everything about one particular part of Python, first try Python's help function, its introspection features, and its online documentation. Each of these is introduced later in this project. You can also try some of the reference manuals. They're different from instructional books (which is what this is). This book: filled with wildly interesting information and humor. Reference manuals: filled with boring (but useful and sometimes important) details. You can also try one of the Python *cookbooks* (a book with coding recipes that solve specific problems).

I walk you through programming

The projects try to show you realistic programming without boring you to tears. When you write your own code to solve your own problems, you'll need methods and approaches *(tools)* that get the job done. I teach you these tools by walking you through each project, step by step. Try every step — don't skip any.

If you want to *run* the working program, skip to the end of the project and cut and paste. If you want to *learn* Python, then consider each project a journey, not a destination. Work through the projects with me and type them in yourself.

Why this book uses Python 2.7

The Python language is changing from Python 2.7 (sometimes called Python 2) to a new version, called Python 3. This change is taking years to complete. Python 3 is very similar to Python 2, but the two are incompatible — they don't work together. If you write a script that works in Python 2, it isn't guaranteed to work in Python 3 (and vice versa).

Deciding whether to use Python 2 or Python 3 in this book was difficult. I focus on Python 2 (specifically Python 2.7) mainly because I think it still has the best third-party libraries. For example, the Minecraft Pi project at www.dummies.com/go/pythonforkids needs Python 2. If you want to do something productive using Python, and you need to use a third-party module to do it, you'll probably need Python 2. Third-party modules that work with Python 3 often have a version that works with Python 2 support, but the reverse isn't true. This will change over the next couple of years.

The way Python 3 is different from Python 2 is mainly in advanced features. Because of that, even if I based the book on Python 3, I wouldn't cover most of what's new about Python 3.

Finally, Python 2 is part of the *standard install* on Mac OSX computers, which means that this book should be usable by Mac owners without your having to download and install anything. Most Linux comes with Python installed (but make sure you have Python version 2.7).

I am practical

Hopefully, you can use these projects for something in your every-day life. Maybe they'll help with your homework or let you store private notes. I start small and dream big. Please dream big with me while you're getting the concepts in the first projects.

Install Python on Mac OSX

To find and start Python on Mac OSX computers, follow these steps:

1. Press Cmd+spacebar to open Spotlight.

2. Type the word `terminal`.

   Or, from the Finder, select Finder ⇨ Go ⇨ Utilities ⇨ Terminal.

   The Terminal window opens.

3. In the terminal, type `python`.

   The Python interpreter that's built in to Mac OSX opens.

Install Python on Windows

Unfortunately, Python doesn't come on Windows. If you're running Windows, then you need to download and install Python by following the instructions here. Installing Python on Windows isn't difficult. If you can download a file from a website, you have the skills to install Python.

Fortunately, the Python Foundation (the peeps who guide the development of Python) makes installable files available from its website.

When I did the installation, I found that Firefox and Internet Explorer responded differently to the Python download website, so the instructions are based on which of these browsers to use. If you use a whole other browser altogether, try the Internet Explorer instructions.

With Firefox

To install Python on a Windows machine with Firefox, follow these steps:

1. Visit www.python.org/downloads.

2. Click the button that says Download Python 2.7.9.

   Or, if it's there, click a more recent version number that starts with 2.7.

   Clicking this button automatically downloads and saves an msi file for you. If not, try the instructions for Internet Explorer. See Figure 1-1.

3. When the download's complete, click the icon for Firefox's download tool.

4. Click the file called python-2.7.9.msi (or the more recent version, if you downloaded one).

   Python 2.7.9 installs on your computer.

With Internet Explorer

To install Python on a Windows machine with Internet Explorer, follow these steps:

1. Visit www.python.org/downloads.

2. From the menu bar, select Downloads ⇨ Windows.

   You can see the menu options in Figure 1-2.

3. Scroll down to the heading Python 2.7.9-2014-12-10.

   Or scroll to a more recent version, which starts with Python 2.7, if one is available.

Internet Explorer

Firefox

Icon for download tool

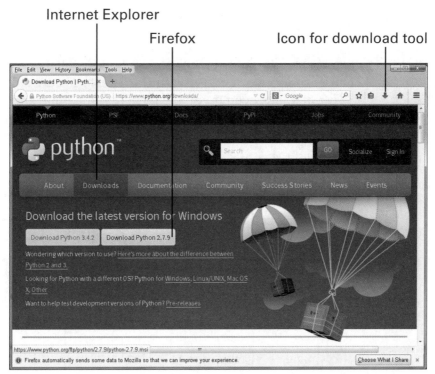

Figure 1-1: Download Python with Firefox.

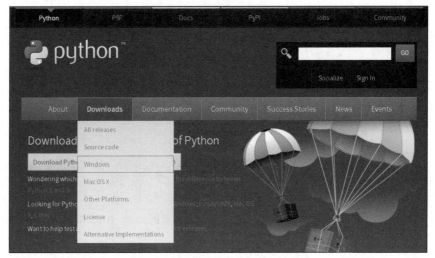

Figure 1-2: Download Python with Internet Explorer.

4. Under this heading, click the link titled `Download Windows x86 MSI Installer`.

See Figure 1-3. This is a link for a 32-bit installation, which makes things work better with third-party libraries. Use the 32-bit installer even if you have a 64-bit machine and even if you have no idea what this paragraph is talking about.

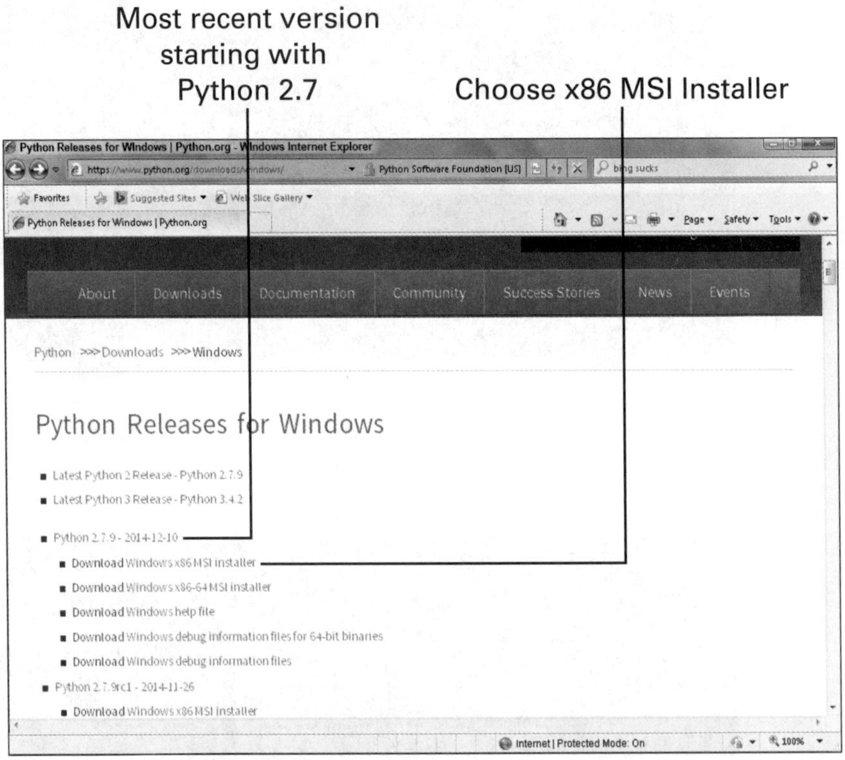

Most recent version
starting with
Python 2.7   Choose x86 MSI Installer

Figure 1-3: Python x86 MSI Installer.

5. If you're asked to choose whether to run or save the file, choose Run.

This downloads `python2.7.9.msi` and starts running the installer.

6. If you get a security warning when the installer begins (or at random times during the installation), choose Run.

7. Accept the default installation options that the installer provides.

Install Python for Linux

If you're running Linux, confirm that you have version 2.7.9 of Python installed, rather than version 3. This shouldn't be a problem because Python 2.7 is installed by default in recent versions of OpenSuSE, Ubuntu, and Red Hat Fedora.

In the nutty odd case when someone has Python 3 but not Python 2.7, read your distribution's documentation for how to use the package manager and get Python 2.7 and IDLE.

Pin Python to Your Start Menu

After you've downloaded Python, it's a good idea to pin it to your Start menu. That way you can find it more easily for the rest of this book.

Type `Python` in the Start menu's search bar, or click All Programs. In the folder `Python 2.7`, you should find the following entries (see Figure 1-4):

- IDLE (Python GUI)

- Module Docs

- Python (command line)

- Python Manuals

- Uninstall Python

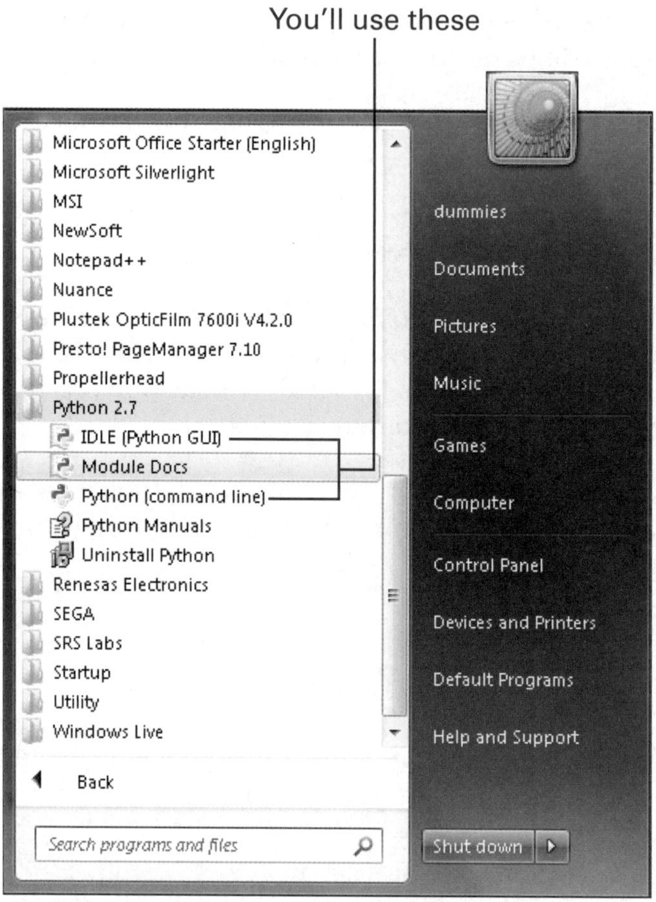

You'll use these

Figure 1-4: Python entries in Start menu.

Of these, you'll use:

✔ IDLE (Python GUI)

✔ Python (command line)

To make IDLE and the command line easier to find, pin them to your Start menu:

1. Open your Start menu.

2. Choose All Programs ➪ Python 2.7.

3. Right-click IDLE (Python GUI). See Figure 1-5.

4. Select Pin to Start Menu.

5. Right-click Python (command line).

6. Select Pin to Start Menu.

You should see the entries at the top of your Start menu. If you prefer, you can pin them to your taskbar.

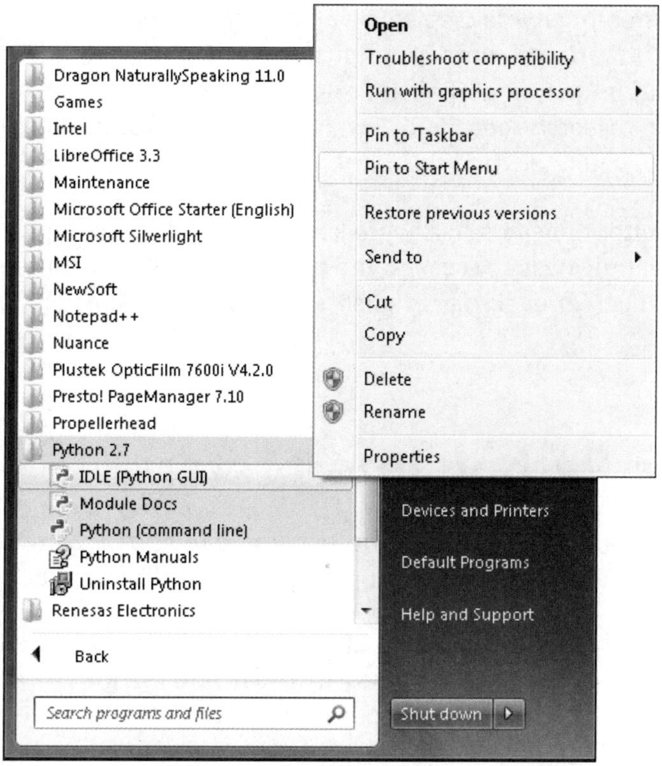

Figure 1-5: Right-click to pin Python to your Start menu.

Python on tablets

Are you interested in running or programming Python using your tablet? If you're interested in writing a program for a tablet, take a look at the Kivy library. I installed SL4A, the Scripting Layer for Android, on my tablet, along with its Python interpreter and drafted some early chapters using SL4A. Check your tablet's app store for Python interpreters and see whether any fit your ability.

Because different tablets display graphics different ways, Python has to use special libraries to write programs other than plain text. Tablets are only useful for the non-graphical projects in this book — unless you're prepared to research those libraries and rewrite the projects to use them. In that case, you're beyond this book.

Also, it's better to have a hardware keyboard. *Soft* (onscreen) keyboards usually don't give easy access to the punctuation that Python needs (or, in my experience, for everyday English — but that's another matter . . .).

Start the Python Interpreter

You can't use this book unless you can start Python. Click Python (command line) that you pinned to your Start menu.

If you haven't pinned it yet, do it. No, seriously. You can also search for Python in the search bar and click Python (command line) in the Programs section of the results.

You get a window that looks like Figure 1-6.

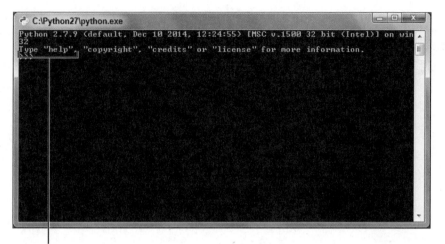

Note this

Figure 1-6: The Python command line suggests you type help if you want help.

Use Python's Built-In Documentation

Python comes with its own help. In fact, in Figure 1-6 it even tells you about it in the welcome message. If you type help and press Enter, you get more help options. Type help() (including the parentheses) to get interactive help like what you see in Figure 1-7.

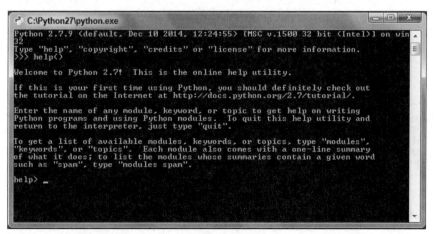

Figure 1-7: Python's interactive help is ready for you to type.

Once you're inside the help service, you can get information on any topic. Just type the topic. The help service can't handle complex queries (like the ones you use to search the Internet), so keep it simple. For example, instead of typing how do I get a range of numbers, type range (and read what it has to say). To quit interactive help, type quit.

You can write help text for your own programs. You do it in Project 5.

Put the Kibosh on the Python Interpreter

You can't use this book unless you can start Python, but you'll want to stop Python after you've started it. If you can't wait to start programming, skip ahead to Project 2.

You can put the kibosh on Python from the command line by doing one of the following:

- ✔ Type exit(), including the parentheses. Press Enter. (This works on any platform; Enter = Return if you're on a Mac.)

- ✔ Click the close icon for the window that Python's running in. (This works on any platform.)

- ✔ On Windows, type Ctrl+Z and then press Enter.

- ✔ On Linux and Mac, type Ctrl-D.

If you're on a Mac, make sure you're using the Ctrl key, not the command key. Also, anytime I mention the Enter key, this means the Return key for you.

Find Python Documentation Online

As I mention, this book doesn't cover every single possible potential thing you could do with Python. I just can't do that in a single book.

Instead, this book *exposes* you to programming in Python. Sort of like the measles. Use this book as a starting point. If you want more information, you should check out

✏ Python's online documentation

✏ Python's introspection features

✏ Professor Internet

✏ Source code (not so much)

Python's online documentation

The Python documentation pages are available at `https://docs.python.org/2.7/`. The most helpful sections are listed here:

✏ The Python language reference at
   `https://docs.python.org/2.7/reference/index.html`

✏ The Python standard library documentation at
   `https://docs.python.org/2.7/library/index.html`

In the left sidebar of the documentation page is a quick search field; you can see it in Figure 1-8. Type your question there and Python will search the documentation for you. It works better if you know the Python keyword, module, or error that you're interested in.

The documentation shows the feature you looked for and a code template for how to use the feature. (See this book's Introduction for how to read code templates.) These docs have a lot of information, but they assume you know how programmers write documentation. This often makes them hard to understand.

Reading the Python documentation is a skill that you have to master if you want to become a Python master. At the moment, though, don't worry that it seems like it's written in a foreign language. Just work through it slowly. As you read more of it, you'll be able to get more information from it. Soon, docs you couldn't understand at all will become mind-numbingly boring. Then you'll know you're making progress!

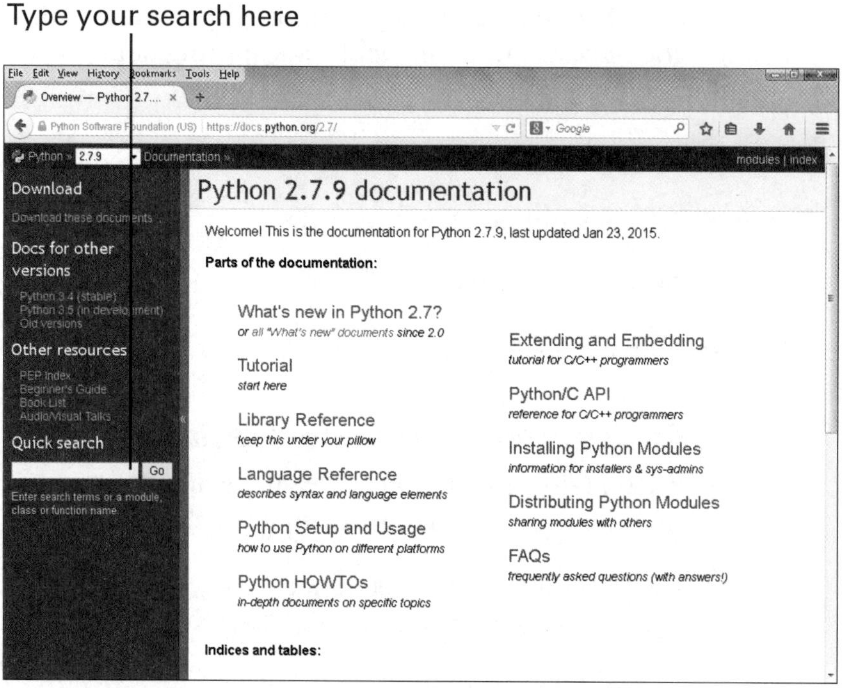

Type your search here

Figure 1-8: Python's online documentation can help.

Python's introspection features

The second form of help is Python's introspection features. *Introspection* means that the program can tell you about itself. Introspection has a lot of different parts. You've already met one of them — the `help` feature. To understand the others you need to know more about Python, so I introduce the rest as you work your way through the book.

Professor Internet

What I like to call "Professor Internet" is the third form of help. When you search the Internet, make sure you include `Python` as one of your search terms, followed by the thing you're wondering about. If you know that it's part of or related to something else, then include that other thing as a search term as well. For example, don't search for `print`, because that's too broad. Search instead for `python print`. (Capitalization won't matter.) Another example is if you were interested in the `Button` widget of the

`Tkinter` toolset (which you meet at `dummies.com/go/ pythonforkids`) you'd search for `python button tkinter`.

You use a different search strategy online from what you need for the interactive help.

If ads are in your results, skip them.

Source code

Source code is the final form of help. Keep in mind that Python is an interpreted language. This means that what you read is what the computer executes. As a result, if you want to know how some third-party module does something (the Python core isn't written in Python, so that won't help), you can literally look at it and see exactly how it did it. You won't understand it at first, but no matter. Dive in. It starts making sense after a while.

Join the Broader Python Community

Check out the Python community that's out there. Look for Internet forums related to Python. The Stackoverflow website (`http://stackoverflow.com/questions/tagged/python`) is helpful when I'm figuring out problems.

Often, an Internet search will turn up questions that someone else has already asked. If you know the answer to a question, answer it. If you're correct, and thorough, you'll get a good reputation.

Don't guess at an answer. Only post if you're sure. Also, don't give your personal information to anyone online. Stick to the topic of programming.

PEPs

Python changes, or *evolves,* when you use proposal documents called Python Enhancement Proposals (known as PEPs). Each PEP proposes some change to Python; the change is either used or ignored. They may provide you some history about how one feature or another was added to Python.

You can ignore most PEPs, but do check out the following two when you're ready to move on from the projects in this book:

- ✔ **PEP 8, Style Guide for Python Code** has rules about how to format your Python code. For example, it suggests the amount of indent for code blocks (see Project 2). It also has rules (called *conventions*) for naming. I did my best to follow PEP 8 rules in this book, but sometimes the lines are longer than they recommend.

- ✔ **PEP 257, Docstring Conventions** sets different conventions relating to docstrings. Docstrings explain, in normal language, what a program (or part of one) is doing. You meet docstrings in Project 5.

 You don't have to follow (*comply* with) with PEPs, but try to. It makes it easier for other people to read your code. Heck, it makes it easier for you to read your code. My earlier Python code isn't PEP 8 compliant, and going back to it is a real pain. Simple things like capital letters in a name make a difference.

Planet Python and PyCon

Planet Python (`http://planetpython.org`) puts together lots of blogs that are Python related. Many of the posts may be hard to understand as a beginner, but like everything else, stick with it — they'll become clear. A lot of top-notch Python programmers have their blogs on Planet Python. You can learn heaps from keeping an eye on them. I have.

Python programmers regularly get together at conferences around the world. These conferences *(confs)* are called PyCon, and their location is added to the name. For example, the one in Australia is called PyCon-AU. See `www.pycon.org` for a list of locations.

I'm not suggesting you hop a plane to Australia to attend PyCon-AU (or even attend one that's close to you). However, I *am* suggesting you hop online and check out the videos from these confs. The videos from various PyCons appear over time at `http://pyvideo.org`. Go there, browse, find something that looks interesting, and watch. It's a great way to get a quick intro-duction (or an in-depth look) at something new.

If you can find them, look at the slide decks for PyCon talks. The slide decks are a little harder to find, but easier to download and review. Look at them first. I often just go off the slide decks, but you might decide to download the video too.

Handle Problems

There are two main kinds of errors:

- A *syntax* error basically means you made a punctuation mis-take. These are the most common errors. Get used to reading what you've typed very closely and comparing it carefully to what you *should* have typed.

If you have trouble getting one of the code examples to run properly, the first thing to do is make sure that you've retyped the code exactly as it's written.

- *Logic* errors occur where you've misunderstood what you're trying to do or what you've asked Python to do. These errors can be difficult to spot and more difficult to track down. Compare the output that you actually get to the output you *ought* to get. This means that you need some way of working out the output that you ought to be receiving. Project 6 shows a logic error and the steps to identify and resolve one.

When Python runs into an error, it tries to give you a clue about what went wrong and where. Try to figure out Python's message. It will usually give you a good place to start.

Sometimes you get an error because you've assumed something that is incorrect. If you can't see what's wrong, think about the assumptions you've made. If you're not making any progress, do something else and reset your brain. Go drink some water, feed Fluffy, or stand up and walk around. Do something that gets your mind on something else, but doesn't steal your brain. (Hopping onto Instagram isn't a good idea, for example.) When you've finished that, come back to your Python problem. Fresh eyes and a fresh mind will help you see the problem differently and hopefully lead to a solution.

If all else fails, bring Fluffy (or your dog, or goldfish, or your pet rock) nearby when you're coding. If you come to a problem you can't solve, stop what you're doing and explain the problem to your pet or object.

Explaining things out loud is an old *debugging* (error fixing) technique. It works because, in order to explain the problem to someone else, you have to first understand it yourself.

You need to *express your problem using words because this causes a different part of your brain to kick in and you think differently about the problem.* If you're like me and you're not the talking type, keep a programming journal. The concept is still the same — write out an explanation of the problem in your journal and why you can't crack it. I promise you this will help you solve many difficult problems.

Learn How to Learn

Reading books isn't enough. You have to *do*. Be the book, feel the book, become one with . . . . (Scratch that last bit. I was channeling a movie there for a second.)

Do

Seriously. You need to actually *do* things if you want to learn. No one ever learned anything by simply reading. It's true of Python, and it's true of anything else you want to learn.

Do the code as you read the book. Don't just cut and paste. Type the whole thing in again yourself, at least for the early projects. That way, you read the code that's been written and somewhat understand why it's been written that way. Copying and pasting won't get you close to the code. Go on. Snuggle up. Freestyle it if you want to add your own changes. You learn faster if you add your own stuff. Own the code!

Make mistakes

If you do, you're gonna whoops. If you're freestyling, don't worry about breaking your code or getting things wrong. (Use Save As to make backups.)

Everyone who writes code gets it wrong the first time. Their logic is wrong; they misspell something. Whatever.

Making mistakes is as important as doing.

This is totally normal. In fact, writing programs is a process, and it has wrong turns and setbacks. Professional programmers make mistakes every day. That doesn't bother them because they code in small pieces that they can handle, and they test what they do.

Think

When you get something wrong, or your code doesn't work like you expected, take the time to understand why. If you think long and hard enough, you'll work it out.

Getting things wrong isn't enough to teach you. It's part of a path to thinking and understanding. That's where the learning comes from. See how it all builds on itself? Sort of like Python.

Ganbatte Ne!

The Japanese have a most excellent word — *ganbatte*. It means a whole heap of different things like cheer up, good luck, do your best, be strong, keep at it, keep your chin up, be courageous, don't give up, and you can do it. When you start learning a pro-gramming language, you have big dreams but small skills. It can feel even tougher because the examples of computer programs you see were made by teams of people working for months on end. Plus, a lot of what makes programs seem special these days is graphic artists, and that's a whole new ballgame!

Hang in there! Your effort will be rewarded.

Summary

In this project you:

- ↙ Saw where and how you can use Python

- ↙ Discovered the two versions of Python and why this book uses Python 2.7

- ↙ Installed Python on your computer, started it, and stopped it

- ↙ Met Python's built-in help and its online documentation

- ↙ Were briefly introduced to the Python community

Hello World!

In Project 1, you install Python and fire up the interpreter. Project 2 gets you into Python proper, transforming you from an ordinary member of the public into a full Python programmer in training.

Tradition dictates that Hello World! be the first program that you write when you're learning a new programming language. You're following in the footsteps of many great programmers when you create this project.

In this project you see how to communicate information from the program to the user by making *(outputting)* a simple message. You see how Python remembers information and how you can name the information that you've asked Python to remember. This means you can reuse the information in other parts of your program.

You'll see how Python makes its way through your programs, how to stop a program if it goes nuts, and how to make a program go a little nuts (to test how to stop it). Finally, check out some core program techniques (called *loops*), which you'll use to cover the screen with greetings.

Write `Hello World!`

To create your Hello World! program, follow these steps:

1. Open your Start menu and choose Python (command line).

You pinned it to the menu in Project 1. You should get a prompt that looks like >>>.

Code listings in this book are formatted in a `different font` to show you that they're Python code.

At the moment, you're doing everything in *interactive mode* in the Python interpreter. That's where the >>> comes in. Python shows you >>> when you're supposed to type something.

2. At the prompt, type the following. Use a single quote at the start and the end — it's beside the Enter key:

```
print('Hello World!')
```

3. Press the Enter key.

Python runs the code you typed.

You see the output shown in Figure 2-1. Congratulations — you've written your first program. Welcome to the Python-programmers-in-training club.

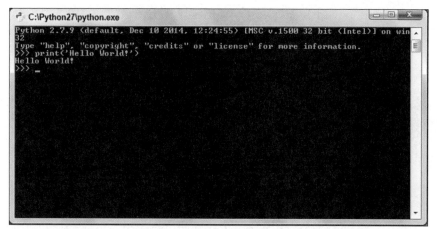

Figure 2-1: Your Hello World! program is ready for more instructions.

If you don't see what's in Figure 2-1, check that you typed in the text from Step 2 exactly as it's written:

- ✓ Check that the parentheses and single quotes are in the right places.

- ✓ Check that for each opening parenthesis there is a closing parenthesis. (Otherwise, you're left hanging.)

- ✓ Check that for each opening quote there's a closing quote.

Programming languages have their own grammar and punctuation rules. These rules are the language's *syntax.* Humans, can work most stuff out even if perfect not you're is grammar (See? You figured out what I was trying to say), but Python pretty much freaks out if you get the syntax wrong.

Spot and Fix Errors

The Python interpreter takes in each line and operates on it immediately (more or less) after you press the Enter key. In Hello World! you use Python's print feature. print takes what's inside the parentheses and outputs it to the command line (also called the *console*).

Python is sensitive to both the grammar and punctuation. If you misspell something, the program won't work. If Python is expecting special characters and you don't put them in, then Python will fail. Some Python issues are shown here. Can you work out how you would fix them?

```
>>> pritn('Hello World!')
Traceback (most recent call last):
  File "<stdin>", line 1, in <module>
NameError: name 'pritn' is not defined
```

Here's another:

```
>>> print('Hello World!)
  File "<stdin>", line 1
    print('Hello World!)
SyntaxError: EOL while scanning string literal
```

Here's another:

```
>>> print 'Hello World!')
  File "<stdin>", line 1
    print 'Hello World!')
                       ^
SyntaxError: invalid syntax
```

Python tries to give you the reason it failed (that is, `NameError` and `SyntaxError`).

Check each of these things:

- All commands are correctly spelled (fail 1)

- Every opening quote mark has a matching closing quote mark (fail 2)

- Every opening parenthesis has a closing parenthesis (fail 3)

Using `print` from Python 2 versus `print()` from Python 3

The `print()` that you used for your first program in this project doesn't need the parentheses. Python 2 has a different `print` syntax from Python 3. In Python 2, `print` is a keyword. Before Python 3 came along, the Hello World! program was pretty easy and looked like this:

```
print "Hello World!"
```

This program doesn't have parentheses. For whatever reason that people in charge do what they do, the Python Software Foundation changed the Python 3 syntax to require the parentheses. When you're coding, remember to put parentheses around what you want to print.

For the code in this book, `print` will work even if you leave the parentheses out. (Don't believe me? Go ahead. Try it.) Because Python 3's syntax *requires* parentheses, I'm using them here so you'll be used to them when you switch to Python 3.

Work with Literals

In Hello World!, the message that `print` is sending is called a *literal*. Think of a literal as being something within single quotes. (Single quotes are this ' instead of double quotes, like this ").

Literals are the rocks (not rock stars) of the programming world. You can pick them up and throw them around, but you can't change them. They can exist by themselves in a program, but they don't do anything:

```
>>> 'Hello World!'
'Hello World!'
```

That's a program that has only a literal and nothing else. It's just a little bit different from the Hello World! program. In that program there were no quotes in the text that Python printed, but in this example the second line has single quote marks around it.

Python doesn't *judge the content* of a literal. That means you can misspell it, fill it with weird words, and even fill it with weird, misspelled words. You still won't get an error message from Python.

The single quotes *are* important. If you leave them out, Python thinks the text is telling it to do something. In this example, Python doesn't know what Hello and World are supposed to do:

```
>>> Hello World!
  File "<stdin>", line 1
    Hello World!
              ^
SyntaxError: invalid syntax
```

The literals mentioned here are all string literals. *String literals* are read like text, instead of like a number. (I don't know why they are called string literals and not something else, like alphabetical literals.)

You can make a sequence of characters into a string literal by putting a single quote on each side:

Hello World! → 'Hello World!'

However, watch what happens when you make a literal from something that already has a single quote (like the word didn't):

```
>>> 'didn't'
  File "<stdin>", line 1
    'didn't'
          ^
SyntaxError: invalid syntax
```

Python reaches the second single quote and thinks that it marks the end of the string literal — but that's not where you wanted it to end.

You can make a literal that includes a single quote by using double quotes around the outside of the literal. You can use double quotes any time, even if there isn't a single quote involved.

```
>>> "didn't"
"didn't"

>>> '"I have a very eely hovercraft," he said.'
'"I have a very eely hovercraft," he said.'
```

Ways you can create string literals include such diverse elements as single quotes and double quotes. But that's not all! You can also use triple single quotes and triple double quotes to create string literals. Seriously:

```
>>> '''This is a literal made with triple single quotes.'''
'This is a literal made with triple single quotes.'

>>> """This is a literal made with triple double quotes [sic]."""
'This is a literal made with triple double quotes [sic].'
```

Make sure you can create at least one literal that has a single quote, one that has a double quote, and one that has both a single quote and a double quote.

Literally Save Your Strings in Variables

Okay, so you're a master maker of string literals. After Python defines a literal, it sort of forgets it (like you might forget to do your chores). Python stores literals in memory then thinks they aren't being used so throws them out in a process called *garbage collection*. (No, I'm not making that up.) Sort of like when you leave something on the floor and it gets thrown in the trash because someone thinks you're not using it.

How do you stop Python from thinking your literal isn't being used? Put a name to your literal. Then Python won't throw it in the garbage. It's sort of like taping a piece of paper to it with "Mine!" written on it.

You name a literal like this:

1. Think up a name that follows the rules *(criteria)* listed after these steps.

2. Put the name on the left side of an equals sign (=).

3. Put the literal on the right side of the equals sign.

Here are a couple of sample names:

```
>>> my_message = 'Hello World!'
>>> my_second_message = 'This name is a little long. Ideally, try to keep
                the name short, but not too short.'
```

Each name you use must *comply* with (follow) these rules:

- It should describe what the literal will be used for. For example, `text_for_question` is a good name for a literal that has the text for a question (if you're asking the user something). But `another_var` is a bad name for it, because it doesn't describe the variable.

- Start it with a letter or an underscore. (Beginning with an underscore, which is _, has a special meaning. You can avoid it for now.)

- It can have underscores (and should usually be made of only lowercase letters and underscores).

- It can have numbers.

- It can have uppercase letters (but just because it can doesn't mean you should; avoid uppercase letters in literal names).

- It can't have a space.

- It can't be the same as any Python keyword. (This project has a list of keywords.)

Use a name to refer to what you've named. Each time you use a name (except on the left side in an assignment), Python acts like you've retyped in full the value that's referenced by the name.

A *value* is something that's referenced by a name. In the earlier examples, the only values are literals. You'll see different kinds of values in the later projects.

Whenever you give a name to a literal (or any other value), you're making an *assignment*. In my_message = 'Hello World!' the value 'Hello World!' is assigned to the name my_message.

You could rewrite your Hello World! program like this:

```
>>> my_message = "Hello World!"
>>> print(my_message)
Hello World!
```

This assigns the name my_message to the literal "Hello World!". (Remember, the name goes on the left side of the equals sign and the literal goes on the right side of the equals sign.) Then prints the literal that you named my_message.

When you've created a name, you can change *what* it names by using the same naming process for a different literal. Or, use another name (since referencing the name is the same as retyping it). To refresh your memory, this is the code from earlier in the project:

```
>>> my_message = 'Hello World!'
>>> my_second_message = 'This name is a little long.  Ideally, try to
            keep the name short, but not too short.'
```

Now, bend your mind and assign the second name to the first name and print it:

```
>>> my_message = my_second_message
>>> print(my_message)
This name is a little long.  Ideally, try to keep the name short,
            but not too short.
```

```
>>> my_message = 'A third message'
>>> print(my_message)
A third message
>>> print(my_second_message)
This name is a little long.  Ideally, try to keep the name short,
               but not too short.
>>> my_message = 'Hello World!'
```

Did you notice that by *varying,* or changing, what something names, you can no longer access what the name pointed to before? No worries. One of the most useful things about computers is that you can vary names this way. Because they can be varied, they're called *variables.* Thus, you'd say that my_message is (the name of) a variable and the value of the variable is "Hello World!". Setting or varying the value of a variable is called *assignment.*

Also notice that the value of my_second_message didn't change. The only thing that changed during an assignment is the variable name on the left side of the equals sign.

You can assign numbers to variables and add, subtract, and compare them:

```
>>> a = 1
>>> b = 2
>>> print(a)
1
>>> print(b)
2
>>> print(a+b)
3
>>> print(b-a)
1
>>> print(a<b)
True
```

This example uses very short names indeed! The symbol < means *less than.* a<b is asking Python whether it's true or false that a is less than b. In this case, a is 1 and b is 2. a is less than b, so Python identifies this as true, and prints True.

You can even refer to the same variable on both sides of the equals sign to change what the variable is holding. For example, to increase the variable a by 1, you'd do (using the value a=1 from the preceding code):

```
>>> a = a+1
>>> print(a)
2
```

Here, Python looks up the value of a, increases it by 1, then stores it back in the variable.

Interrupt a Program

Usually you get called rude if you interrupt. Not here. Are you ready to create a program that never finishes by itself (called an *infinite loop*)? This section shows you how to force it to stop.

Forcing a stop is useful when your program locks up and won't respond. The trick is to press Ctrl+C (the Ctrl key and the C key at the same time; *don't* press the Shift key). Make sure the Python window is active (by clicking the window) when you do — or you might close the wrong program!

Here's how you write an infinite loop program:

1. Type while True: and press Enter.

2. Press the spacebar four times.

3. Type pass.

4. Press Enter twice.

This is what you'll see:

```
>>> while True:
...        pass
...
```

What's with the dots?

When you run Python (command line) you're in Python's *interactive mode*. Python responds immediately or interactively to what you type. When you're in interactive mode on the Python interpreter, you get a prompt that looks like . . . or >>>. You've already met >>>. What . . . means is that Python is expecting a new code block from you and will keep accepting new lines until you press Enter twice in a row.

You can add as many statements to a code block as you like, but make sure they're all indented by the same amount. Python coding conventions suggest four spaces.

The Python interpreter is unresponsive. If you try to get it to assign or print something, nothing happens. It lays there like a lump. The usual >>> prompt isn't there. You may also hear your computer laboring.

Quick: Press Ctrl+C to break out of the loop and get control back. You get this when you do it:

```
>>> while True:
...     pass
...
^CTraceback (most recent call last):
  File "<stdin>", line 1, in <module>
KeyboardInterrupt
>>>
```

The `Traceback (most recent call last): File "<stdin>", line 1, in <module> KeyboardInterrupt.` section is called a stack trace or a backtrace. A *stack trace* gives you information about what happened just before a program ran into an error. In complex programs, the stack tells where else it was in the program before the error occurred.

Did you notice the `while` statement in this code block? The `while` statement repeatedly *executes* (runs) a code block while a condition is satisfied.

A *condition* is any formula that has an answer of either `True` or `False`. If the formula is true, then the condition is satisfied. Otherwise, it's not. In this example the condition was just `True`, which is, you know, true. So the condition is always satisfied.

There is another example in the following code. When you're typing it, you must

1. Press the spacebar four times before you type `a = a+1`.

2. Press the spacebar four times before you type `print(a)`.

3. Press Enter twice after `print(a)`.

What's happening here? The numbers from 3 to 10 print out. Python runs `print(a)` eight times (count them!), even though the program only has one `print` statement.

```
>>> a = 2
>>> while a < 10:
...         a = a+1
...         print(a)
...
3
4
5
6
7
8
9
10
```

The first thing Python encounters in this example is the `while` keyword. This keyword tells Python to keep repeating the next block of code `while` a condition is true. In this case the condition is a < 10. The code block is the two lines a= a+1 and `print(a)`. How can you tell this is the code block? First, the colon tells Python "I am about to give you a code block." Second, Python defines its code blocks by whether the indentation of the code lines up. Since both of these lines are indented by four spaces, they are considered the same code block.

Generally speaking, Python moves through your code from top to bottom, performing each instruction in the order it encounters it. In some cases it will repeat certain sections of your code. This is what Python does with `while`. You *can* jump from one part of your code to another, but the code always goes to the next piece of code from the top.

When Python first enters the code block that you just created, the variable a had been set to the value 2. It increased by 1 in the first line of the code block (a = a+1), so the first printed value is 3. The code block ends when Python has finished this `print`. Python then goes back to the top of the block and checks the inequality condition. Since a is now 3 (and less than 10), the code block repeats — a increases to 4 and is printed. This continues until a reaches 9. When a equals 10, then a is no longer less than 10. The condition (a < 10) isn't satisfied and Python stops processing the `while`.

This structure is called a *loop* (in this case a *while loop*) because Python loops through the statement's code block *while* the condition remains true.

The first `while` loop was very short, but made the computer work after a little while (no pun intended). It looked like this:

```
>>> while True:
...     pass
```

This was the first multiline program you entered into the interpreter. It also didn't seem to do anything. That's largely because it used the `pass` keyword.

The pass keyword tells Python to pass over this line. It's a bit odd to include an instruction that doesn't do anything, don't you think? pass is there because when Python sees a keyword like while, sooner or later it runs into a colon (which looks like this :). This colon signals to Python that it's about to get a block of code. The interpreter complains if it doesn't get a code block like it's expecting.

See for yourself how upset it gets:

```
>>> while True:
...
    File "<stdin>", line 2

          ^

IndentationError: expected an indented block
```

 The pass keyword is mainly there to keep the Python interpreter happy while you're planning your program. It also serves as a visual marker for you when you're coding.

Drive Up to Python Keywords

Officially, Python has 31 words *keywords:*

'and'	'except'	'lambda'
'as'	'exec'	'not'
'assert'	'finally'	'or'
'break'	'for'	'pass'
'class'	'from'	'print'
'continue'	'global'	'raise'
'def'	'if'	'return'
'del'	'import'	'try'
'elif'	'in'	'while'
'else'	'is'	'with'
	'yield'	

These advanced keywords aren't covered by this book:
`'assert'`, `'del'`, `'except'`, `'exec'`, `'finally'`, `'global'`,
`'raise'`, `'try'`, and `'yield'`.

The main thing to remember is that you can't use a keyword as
the name of a variable. (But it can be part of the name of a variable. For example, `return` can't be the name of a variable, but
`return_value` is okay.)

Try to assign something to the keyword `return` and you'll fail:

```
>>> return = 4
  File "<stdin>", line 1
    return = 4
           ^
SyntaxError: invalid syntax
```

If you get an `invalid syntax` error message when you're trying
to assign a value to a variable, you'll know why.

Many Loop, Much Hello

You can spread greetings of happiness across the screen when
you know about loops. Type this in and add a comma at the end
of a `print` statement (in this case after `print(my_message)`)
and don't forget to press Ctrl+C to stop!

```
>>> my_message = 'Hello World!'
>>> while True:
...        print(my_message),
...
```

What's with the comma? Each time you call `print`, you get a
message. The next time it prints, the output starts on a new line.
When you add a comma at the end of the `print`, the next time it
prints, the output starts from where it left off without adding a
new line.

When I was young, my favorite was something like this. Who am I kidding? Figure 2-2 shows one of my favorite programs now:

```
>>> message = 'Brendan is Awesome!!'
>>> while True:
...         print(message)
...
```

Feel free to put your own name in here. You're awesome too.

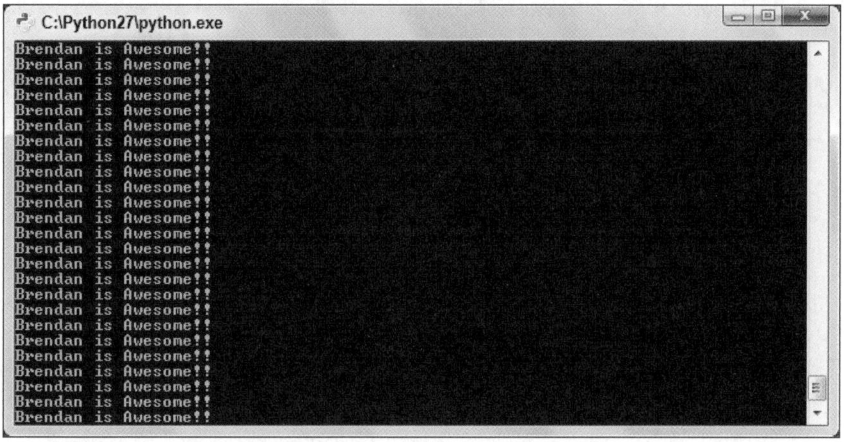

Figure 2-2: Brendan is so awesome.

Fill the Screen with Greetings

It's pretty neat to cover the screen with Hello Worldness, but it's a drag to press Ctrl+C to stop the program. You also run the risk of overtaxing your computer if you let it run too long.

It's better to print the message only a certain number of times. You could do that with the `while` command. But you can use the `range()` command, which is for counting between numbers:

```
>>> range(3)
[0, 1, 2]
```

`range` gives you the numbers from 0 up to — but not including — the number in the parentheses (in this case, 3).

range **versus** xrange

If you're using Python 2.7, the `range` built-in is usually a mistake because it uses more memory than another built-in called `xrange`. Python 3 doesn't have `xrange`, so it's good to get in the habit of using `range` now. Using `range` means your programs will run in Python 3 (and your `range` code will become magically more memory efficient). I also assume that you won't need very large ranges. (Up to `1000` is usually okay.)

Notice that you get the numbers less than the number given to `range`. You might think it's a little strange for `range` to start at 0 instead of 1. You might also think it's strange to leave out the number you want it to count to. Is that madness?

This form of counting (starting from zero) is called *zero-based counting* or numbering. A whole bunch of complicated reasons boil down to "It makes calculating a heap of things easier."

Make Python Count

You can use `range` to count from one number to another if you put the first and last numbers in the parentheses separated with a comma:

```
>>> range(3,10)
[3, 4, 5, 6, 7, 8, 9]
```

Here Python counts from the first number up to — but not including — the second number. It can even count in steps. To do this, you add a third number for the size of each step. To get the odd numbers from 3 up to 10, start at 3 and go to 10 in steps of 2 each:

```
>>> range(3,10,2)
[3, 5, 7, 9]
```

Python counts down if the third number is negative. You need to make the first number bigger than the second, though:

```
>>> range(13,10,-1)
[13, 12, 11]
```

You can *iterate* (take each value in order) through each of the numbers as range counts them:

```
>>> for i in range(3):
...     print(i)
...
0
1
2
```

Because it's a new code block, print(i) has four spaces before it.

This code has the same *structure* (it's built the same) you saw in the while loop, although now there's no conditional. Instead, the for statement names a variable (in this case i). The variable takes the value of each number created by range(3).

The code block repeats for each of the numbers 0, 1, and 2 (although the code block in this case is only a single line of code — print(i)). You can give the variable any name, but it's a *throwaway* variable with no meaning outside the loop, so something short is preferable. Certainly don't give it the same name as another variable or use a variable that is storing something important.

Try to have meaningful names for your variables. (These dummy variables are an exception to that rule.)

Be aware that on each loop iteration, the value of the dummy variable changes. That's why the dummy variable should be just that — a throwaway that's only used in the code block defined by the for loop. (When you're really experienced, you can bend this rule to suit your needs.)

Programmers use the letters i, j, and k for dummy variables that are counting in a loop (usually a for loop). A variable like this is called a *counter* or an *index*.

You can use a dummy variable to change the infinite while loop so it runs only enough times to fill the screen. Then it stops.

```
>>> my_message = "Hello World!"
>>> for i in range(300):
...        print(my_message),
...
```

You should see something like Figure 2-3.

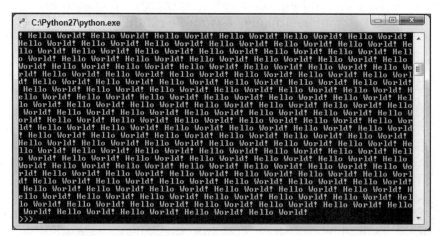

Figure 2-3: 300 x Hello World!

The number 300 in this listing is called a *magic number* because it seems to appear out of nowhere, for no apparent reason, in the middle of your code. Magic numbers are generally a bad idea. When you use a number in a program, it's better to assign the number to a variable. Since you're using meaningful variable names, it's clear what the meaning of the number is. Then use the variable where you were going to use the number.

In this case you'd add NUMBER_OF_HELLOS = 300 earlier and change the range entry to be range(NUMBER_OF_HELLOS). This makes no difference in a three-line program, but it matters as your programs grow.

You might not think you'll need to change these numbers, but you often do (for example, several times during the whole of your development). If they're *inlined* as numbers everywhere (that is, not assigned to a variable and referenced through the variable) in your code, then you have to find and change each one. Plus, since it's a number, it has none of the context that it would have if it was assigned to a variable with a meaningful name; it's not always clear that it's right to change it.

You might, for example, have another part of the code where you want to include 300 units of space. You decide that it should be 100 units of space instead, so you use search and replace to make every 300 a 100. If you've inlined these numbers, then you also wind up changing the 300 in the range and breaking your code.

But, if you stored these values in variables NUMBER_OF_HELLOS = 300 and AMOUNT_OF_SPACE= 300, you only have to change the assignment (AMOUNT_OF_SPACE= 100). Then each and every place where the variable is referenced is automatically updated; other variables with the same value (for example, AMOUNT_OF_ SPACE = 300) aren't changed.

Summary

In this project, you:

- ✔ Read what a literal is.

- ✔ Assigned values to names and created a variable with that name. (Technically you're creating names. The word *variable* is a holdover from other programming languages.)

- ✔ Met five keywords (`for`, `in`, `pass`, `print`, `while`), one value (`True`), and one "built-in" (`range`).

- ✔ Stopped a runaway program with Ctrl+C.

Week 2
Building Guessing Games

This week you're . . .

Guessing Game

Guess what? You're going to create a game where the computer chooses a number and the player guesses the number.

This project teaches you how to get input from the user and how numbers work in Python (they're different from strings). You create a random number and in the process reuse someone else's code in your own projects. You also do a little bit of debugging and tracking down logical errors.

```
C:\Python27\python.exe                                    _ □ X
...
What is your guess? 97
Too high
What is your guess? 6
Too low
What is your guess? 82
Too high
What is your guess? 23
Too low
What is your guess? 64
Too high
What is your guess? 46
Too high
What is your guess? 35
Too low
What is your guess? 40
Too high
What is your guess? 37
Too low
What is your guess? 39
Too high
What is your guess? 38
Correct!
>>>
>>>
```

Plan the Game

In the guessing game, Python thinks of a random number. The player guesses the number.

> If the player guesses correctly, Python says so.
>
> If the player guesses incorrectly, Python says whether the number is higher or lower.
>
> The player keeps guessing until the player gets the right number.

If you did Project 2, you already know how to tell the player something — that's what `print` is for. However, what you don't know about the game at the moment is how to get Python to think of a random number, or how to get a guess from the player.

This cycle — output, input, then input processing — is common structure for many computer programs.

Get Input from the Player

In practice, your program will always need some kind of input from the user. You're still using the command line right now, so text is the only way to get input. You get text from a user by using a special built-in called `raw_input`. It waits for the user to type something and returns to Python what the user types.

Open a Python (command line) prompt by clicking the Python (command line) application that you pinned to your Start menu in Project 1 and try it now:

1. Type `raw_input()` at the prompt.

2. Press Enter.

   You get a blank line.

3. Type a response.

4. Press Enter.

What you typed in Step 1 will echo back to you:

```
>>> raw_input()
I am typing a response. Python won't see this until I press Enter.
"I am typing a response. Python won't see this until I press Enter."
```

When you type your response and press Enter, whatever you typed is echoed back to the terminal surrounded by single or double quotes. Python was echoing your literals the same way when you entered literals in Project 2. Does this give you an idea how to capture input?

In the printout `"This is me typing a response. Python won't see this until I press Enter."`, double quotes echo my input. This is because I included a ' (`won't`) in my response.

Ask for Input

You can make `raw_input()` friendlier by giving it a literal. `raw_input()` prints the literal to the screen before getting the player's response. In this code, `"What is your guess?"` is the literal.

A line starting with `>>>` or `. . .` means that you need to type the rest of the text on that line.

```
>>> raw_input("What is your guess?")
What is your guess?17
'17'
```

Python does exactly what you tell it to do, and in this case that's not so great. It doesn't insert a space between your string prompt and where the player starts typing. To make it friendlier still, insert your own space at the end of the prompt.

```
>>> raw_input("What is your guess? ")
What is your guess? 17
'17'
```

The literal name is between the parentheses. You could replace the name with a variable pointing to a literal:

```
>>> prompt = 'What is your guess? '
>>> raw_input(prompt)
What is your guess? 17
'17'
```

Including a space at the end of the string makes the player's response easier to read.

How do you capture what the user types? Well, you do the same as you do for any other literal — you name it. In the following code, it's named `players_guess`.

```
>>> prompt = 'What is your guess? '
>>> players_guess = raw_input(prompt)
What is your guess? 17
>>>
>>> players_guess
'17'
```

The number `17` isn't echoed immediately because it has been stored in the variable named `players_guess`. That means you can use that response later in your program.

Make Sure Things Are Equal

Your game needs to check whether the guess is the same as the computer's number. This is a kind of *comparison*. If you want to test whether `a` is equal to 1, you can't write `if a= 1:` because the equals sign assigns a value to a variable. Python would read this as "if take the value 1 and give it the name a." Python rightly objects that this is nonsense.

Python uses a special symbol to test whether two things are equal. That symbol is two equals signs together, like this: ==. To test whether the name a contains the value 1 you would type: a == 1. Try it yourself:

```
>>> a = 1
>>> a == 1
True
>>> a = 2
>>> a == 1
False
```

Just to reinforce the point that = means an assignment, try these:

```
>>> 1 == 1
True
>>> 1 == 2
False
>>> 1 = 2
  File "<stdin>", line 1
SyntaxError: can't assign to literal
```

The first and third lines of code ask Python if 1 is equal to 1 (1 == 1) and if 1 is equal to 2 (1 == 2). In the fifth line you're telling Python to take the value 2 and store it in the value 1 (1 = 2).

You get a syntax error because 1 isn't (and can't be) the name of a variable. You can see that the error text explains that Python can't assign to literal.

When Python sees ==, it compares the value on the left against the value on the right. If they're equal, Python replaces the entire statement with the value True. If they aren't equal, Python replaces the entire statement with the value False.

Call the Operators

The equals sign and doubled equals sign are called *operators*. They work, or operate, on the things on either side of them. Table 3-1 has more common operators. Whenever you want to compare, add, subtract, and so on, use an operator. You need them a lot.

Table 3-1		Common Python Operators	
Operator	Name	Effect	Examples
+	Plus	Add two numbers. Join two strings together.	Add: `>>> 1+1` `2` Join: `>>> 'a'+'b'` `'ab'`
–	Minus	Subtract a number from another. Can't use for strings.	`>>> 1-1` `0`
*	Times	Multiply two numbers. Make copies of a string.	Multiply: `>>> 2*2` `4` Copy: `>>> 'a'*2` `'aa'`
/	Divide	Divide one number by another. Can't use for strings. Python uses / because there's no ÷ on your keyboard.	Ermagaaard! It's complicated. See the next section.
%	Remainder (Modulo)	Give the remainder when dividing the left number by the right number. Formatting operator for strings. (See Project 8.)	`>>> 10%3` `1`
**	Power	x**y means raise x to the power of y. Can't use for strings.	`>>> 3**2` `9`

Operator	Name	Effect	Examples
=	Assign-ment	Assign the value on the right to the variable on the left.	`>>> a = 1`

==	Equality	Is the left side equal to the right side? `True` if so; is `False` otherwise.	`>>> 1 == 1`
			`True`
			`>>> 'a' == 'a'`
			`True`

!=	Not equal	Is the left side *not* equal to the right side? `True` if so; is `False` otherwise.	`>>> 1 != 1`
			`False`
			`>>> 1 != 2`
			`True`
			`>>> 'a' != 'A'`
			`True`

>	Greater than	Is the left side greater than the right side? >= means greater than or equal to	`>>> 2 > 1` `True`
<	Less than	Is the left side less than the right side? <= means less than or equal to	`>>> 1 < 2` `True`

& (or and)	And	Are both left and right true?
		Usually for complex conditions where you want to do something if everything is true:
		`while im_hungry`
		`and you_have_`
		`food:`
			`>>> True & True`
			`True`
			`>>> True and False`
			`False`
			`>>> True & (1 == 2)`
			`False`

(continued)

Table 3-1 (Continued)

Operator	Name	Effect	Examples
| (or or)	Or	Is either left or right true?	`>>> True | False` `True`

		Usually for complex conditions where you want at least one thing to be true:
		`while im_bored`
		`or youre_bored:`
			`>>> True or False`
			`True`
			`>>> False | False`
			`False`
			`>>> (1 == 1) |`
			`False`
			`True`

Divide in Python

Division in Python 2.7 is a little complicated. Python tries to be helpful when you divide, but usually it hinders more than helps. The reason is that Python changes the answer if one of your numbers has a decimal point in it.

Python treats decimal numbers — called *floats,* short for *floating point numbers* — differently from numbers that don't have decimals. (A number without a decimal is called an *integer,* a *whole number,* or an *int.*) If you try to divide an integer by an integer in Python 2.7, the answer is rounded down to the nearest integer. Ironic, since it's Python 2.7 and all.

When you want to divide something in Python, use the / operator, like this:

```
>>> 3/2
1
>>> -3/2
-2
```

You didn't get 1.5 or -1.5. You got 1 and -2. You get -2 because Python rounds the negative number -1.5 *down* and the next integer less than -1.5 is -2.

You can avoid rounding by adding a decimal point to either number. Adding the decimal point makes the number a *float*. If Python's operating on a float, it does what you'd expect it to do.

In this exercise make sure you add a dot (a period, full stop, decimal point — whatever you want to call it) after either the 3 or the 2 (or after both):

```
>>> 3/2.
1.5
```

If the number's an integer and is stored in a variable, you don't have anywhere to put your decimal point. In that case, use the float() built-in to convert it to a float, like you see here with 3/float(a):

```
>>> a=2
>>> 3/a
1
>>> 3/float(a)
1.5
>>>
```

Compare the Guess to a Number

Remember this code (you don't need to retype this):

```
>>> prompt = 'What is your guess? '
>>> raw_input(prompt)
What is your guess? 17
'17'
```

When Python echoes the input back, the input is in single or double quotes. This should be a flag to you that Python sees these responses as strings. Python doesn't even see the '17' as a number.

A quick way to test whether Python thinks something is a number is by trying to add a number to it:

```
>>> a=1
>>> a+1
2
```

First you store 1 in a. Then you add 1 to it. No problem, because a has a number in it. However, when you try to add 1 to players_guess:

```
>>> players_guess = raw_input(prompt)
What is your guess? 17
>>> players_guess+1
Traceback (most recent call last):
  File "<stdin>", line 1, in <module>
TypeError: cannot concatenate 'str' and 'int' objects
```

Problem! Something's wrong with players_guess. Python tells you that it "cannot concatenate 'str' and 'int' objects". Python isn't even trying to add them — *concatenate* means to join them. Confirm what players_guess is by printing it out:

```
>>> players_guess
'17'
```

As you expect, players_guess is '17'. (Note the single quotes.) The ones around 17 keep Python from understanding it as a number.

raw_input always returns a string. Whatever the player types, even if it's just a number, you're going to get a string from raw_input. To compare the guess, you need to convert (change) the player's guess into a number.

Say that the computer has come up with 17. To compare the variable `players_input` to this number, follow these steps:

1. Store the value in a variable:

   ```
   >>> computers_number = 17
   ```

2. Compare the player's guess with the number the computer came up with by using the equality operator `==`:

   ```
   >>> computers_number == players_guess
   False
   ```

   This code — `computers_number == players_guess` — asks if 17 is equal to `'17'`. At the moment, the comparison is `False`. That's because the player's guess is still stored as a string and a string is never equal to a number. So the comparison will always be `False`.

3. Convert the player's guess into a number by using the `int()` built-in:

   ```
   >>> computers_number == int(players_guess)
   True
   ```

The `int` built-in takes a string that has a whole number and changes it into something Python recognizes as a number. The `int()` built-in will fail if the string has a decimal number or doesn't have a number. Empty spaces before and after the number are okay.

Here are some examples:

```
>>> int('1.0')
Traceback (most recent call last):
  File "<stdin>", line 1, in <module>
ValueError: invalid literal for int() with base 10: '1.0'
```

You get an error because `1.0` isn't an integer. `int` doesn't know how to convert decimal numbers. In the next example, Python gets confused by the words `fine day` in the string:

```
>>> int('1 fine day')
Traceback (most recent call last):
  File "<stdin>", line 1, in <module>
ValueError: invalid literal for int() with base 10: '1 fine day'
```

Finally, `int` can deal with extra spaces around an otherwise valid number:

```
>>> int('       17      ')
17
```

Compare the Player's Guess to the Computer's Number

When you can compare the guess with the answer, you can print a response for the player.

Remember whenever you're coding:

- ✔ The colon (`:`) means that a new code block is about to follow.

- ✔ On the line after the colon, and every other line in the block, you need to start with four spaces.

Check out this block of code:

```
>>> if computers_number == int(players_guess):
...         print("Correct!")
...
Correct!
```

The `if` statement is here in all its glory. This `if` is another one of Python's keywords. The statement is followed immediately by a condition: Is `computers_number` equal to `players_guess` after it's converted to an integer? This is followed by a colon, also known as "Hey Python, expect a code block."

If the condition is true, Python *executes* (runs) the code block. If it isn't true, Python skips the code block and continues execution at the next statement after the end of the code block. You can think of `if` like an *if . . . then* phrase in English (minus the *then*).

Try the following example, but remember:

✔ Each colon signals that a new code block is about to follow.

✔ On the line after the colon, and every other line in the block, start with four spaces.

```
>>> if 1==2:
...     print("Correct!")
...
>>> if 1==1:
...     print("Correct!")
...
Correct!
```

In the first example, since 1 isn't equal to 2, the `print` statement (`"Correct!"`) was skipped. Nothing happened. If there were more to the code block, the whole code block would be skipped. In the second example, 1 is equal to 1, so the `print` statement is executed. You get a big, juicy `Correct!`

Code blocks

The programming structure — statement, condition, colon, code block — is a very common one in Python. Code blocks are one of the main ways to control flow in a program. *Flow* is the path that the Python interpreter follows as it makes its way through your program. Make sure you know the flow (and go with the flow, too).

Tell Players If the Guess Is Wrong

What happens if the player guesses the wrong answer? Python's got your back on that too.

Always be thinking of how to give players feedback for their actions, even in simple programs.

In the following code block, you see the `if` keyword. The `else` keyword changes the operation of the `if` keyword. Unlike `if`, `else` doesn't take a condition. It's always executed when a preceding `if` code block isn't executed. You use `if`/`else` where you want to execute one of two code blocks, but not both.

The following code continues from where you left off. It assumes that `computers_number = 17` and `players_guess = '17'`.

```
>>> if computers_number == int(players_guess)+1:
...      print('Correct!')
... else:
...      print('Wrong! Guess again')
...
Wrong! Guess again
```

In this code I added `+1` to make the values different on purpose. Otherwise, the `else:` code block won't execute.

You can see that `else` is followed by a colon and — not much of a surprise here — a code block. You know it's a code block because it's indented by four spaces from the indent level of the `else`. (Speaking of indentation: Line up the beginning of the `else` keyword with the beginning of the `if` keyword before it.)

If the `if` condition is `True`, then its code block is executed and the code block following the `else` is ignored. The keyword `else` means "Otherwise, do this stuff." If the condition is `False`, then the code block following the `if` is ignored and the one after the `else` is executed.

Even this doesn't say why the guess is wrong. You have to show players whether the guess is too high or too low.

What you need is a test. (I know, a test is probably the last thing you *really* need.) The test tells players whether they're right on, too low, or too high.

```
>>> if computers_number == int(players_guess):
...         print('Correct!')
... elif computers_number > int(players_guess):
...         print('Too low')
... else:
...         print('Too high')
...
Correct!
```

It turns out `if` has one last trick up its sleeve — `elif`. You use `elif` (short for `else if`) after an `if` to test other things when the first condition isn't satisfied. You can string together as many `elif`s in a row as you like.

For example, suppose you want to do different things if `a` is equal to 1, 2, and 3 respectively. You can use the `elif` structure to test each individually:

```
>>> a = 3
>>> if a == 1:
...         print('a is 1!')
... elif a == 2:
...         print('a is 2!')
... elif a == 3:
...         print('a is 3!')
... else:
...         print("I don't know what a is")
...
a is 3!
```

If you have more than a couple `elif`s in a row, try solving the problem another way instead.

Test that this `elif` structure works. Tell the player when the guess is too high or too low:

```
>>> computers_number = 16
>>> if computers_number == int(players_guess):
...        print('Correct!')
... elif computers_number > int(players_guess):
...        print('Too low')
... else:
...        print('Too high')
...
Too high
>>> computers_number = 18
>>> if computers_number == int(players_guess):
...        print('Correct!')
... elif computers_number > int(players_guess):
...        print('Too low')
... else:
...        print('Too high')
...
Too low
```

Retype that. Yes, really. It's tedious but life will get easier in Project 4. Other things to notice about this code:

- All the `print` statements have the same number of spaces in front of them (indented four spaces or one level).

- All of the `if`, `elif`, and `else` have the same number of spaces in front of them (no indents).

- The computer's number was set lower, then higher, than the guess (17) to test the comparison logic.

- When the computer's number is set lower (16), Python prints that the player's guess is too high.

- When the computer's number is set higher (18), Python prints that the player's guess is too low.

Keep Asking Until the Player Guesses Correctly

Now you know how to ask for the player's guess, how to convert (change) the answer into a number, and how to compare the player's answer to the computer's number.

You still need to set something up so that the computer keeps asking if the player doesn't guess the number. You do this by

- Putting the code that asks for the player's guess and tests its value in a `while` loop.

- Using the `break` statement when the correct answer is given. This lets you *break* out of the loop.

```
>>> computers_number = 17
>>> prompt = 'What is your guess? '
>>> while True:
...         players_guess = raw_input(prompt)
...         if computers_number == int(players_guess):
...             print('Correct!')
...             break
...         elif computers_number > int(players_guess):
...             print('Too low')
...         else:
...             print('Too high')
...
What is your guess? 3
Too low
What is your guess? 93
Too high
What is your guess? 50
Too high
What is your guess? 30
Too high
```

```
What is your guess? 20
Too high
What is your guess? 10
Too low
What is your guess? 19
Too high
What is your guess? 16
Too low
What is your guess? 18
Too high
What is your guess? 17
Correct!
```

The break statement is bold here so you can see it easily. The break statement allows you to exit any loop that Python's already in, regardless of conditions on the enclosing loops. For example, say you have a whole heap of colors and want to see if the red is one of them. You'd set up a loop to run through all the colors. But if you found red halfway through (or even on the first try), there'd be no point continuing. You could use break to stop the loop.

break is also a keyword. (You're barreling through all the keywords you need to know!) Only use it inside a loop:

```
>>> break
    File "<stdin>", line 1
SyntaxError: 'break' outside loop
```

If you have a loop inside a loop, the break applies to the loop level that the break appears in (or its relevant flow control statement, because it's almost always subject to a condition).

Here are some examples of how break works. In the next code excerpt:

✔ The code uses the built-in str(). The str built-in converts a number to a string. You can join strings together using the + operator. (Operators are in Table 3-1 earlier.)

✓ There are two loops — an inner loop on j that counts more quickly, and an outer loop on i that counts more slowly.

✓ The break is encountered when the value of i reaches 1 (up from 0). Since the break is in the inner loop's code block, it only breaks out of the inner loop. You can tell because i keeps counting up to 2, but j resets at 0 when i is 1.

```
>>> for i in range(3):
...     for j in range(3):
...         print(str(i)+", "+str(j))
...         if i == 1:
...             break

0, 0
0, 1
0, 2
1, 0
2, 0
2, 1
2, 2
```

To break the outer loop, you need to be in the outer loop's code block. In particular, the code if i == 1: is indented by four spaces, not eight as in the previous example.

Here, the outer loop stops when i is 1. The outer loop never makes it to 2:

```
>>> for i in range(3):
...     for j in range(3):
...         print(str(i)+", "+str(j))
...     if i == 1:
...         break

0, 0
0, 1
```

```
0, 2
1, 0
1, 1
1, 2
```

Take a moment to think about what's happening with these loops, and try some of your own.

Make Python Think of a Random Number

The player's guessing numbers. How do you get Python to think of a number?

The *random integer* feature `randint` is from the `random` module. It gives you a random number between two numbers that you put in the parenthesis that follows `randint`. The number will include the lowest or highest number. If you want a number between 6 and 10 (inclusive), use `random.randint(6,10)`.

```
>>> import random
>>> random.randint(1,100)
67
>>> help(random.randint)
```

Because this is a new feature, type `help(random.randint)` at the Python prompt and read what it tells you. If you don't get back the `>>>` prompt, press q when you're finished.

```
>>> random.randint(1,100)
15
>>> random.randint(1,100)
72
>>> random.randint(1,100)
25
>>> random.randint(1,100)
36
```

```
>>> random.randint(1,100)
90
>>> random.randint(1,100)
81
>>> random.randint(1,100)
23
```

Simple, huh? See how the number is changing?

But you can't just up and use `random.randint` like you can with built-ins such as `raw_input` and `str`. To use `random.randint`, you must tell Python that you want to use a function from the `random` module — `import random`.

This code example uses a new keyword. The `import` statement makes a module (in this case the `random` module) available to Python. You can use all the features in the module after you import it.

Why would you want to import a module? *Modules* are Python's way of organizing collections of features together. For example, stuff relating to random numbers is in the `random` module. Stuff for math is in the `math` module. Stuff related to dates and times is in the `datetime` module. Stuff for saving your data is in the `pickle` module. (Wait. What?)

You have already met some features — `int`, `range`, and `raw_input`. But you didn't need to `import` anything to use them because they're *built in* to Python (which is why they're called built-ins). They're always available when Python is running.

The `random` module isn't a built-in, so it isn't always available. You get an error if you start a new Python prompt and try `random.randint(1,100)`:

```
Python 2.7.3 (default, Apr 14 2012, 08:58:41) [GCC] on
              linux2
Type "help", "copyright", "credits" or "license" for more
              information.
>>> random.randint(1,100)
```

```
Traceback (most recent call last):
  File "<stdin>", line 1, in <module>
NameError: name 'random' is not defined
```

The `random` module does come with Python, but unlike the built-ins, it isn't loaded automatically. The `random` module is part of the Python standard library. If you need it, you must `import` it.

Why can't Python just automatically load everything? Because it would make programming boring. Every time you ran a program, you'd need to wait while it found and loaded all the modules in the standard library.

Besides giving you access to the standard library, the `import` statement also lets you use modules that someone else has written (called *third-party modules*). To use those, you have to download and install them on your computer.

Python's awesome power

Tie down all moveable objects in your house and tether yourself, your family, and your pets to something solid before using `import antigravity`.

Use Namespaces

The dot syntax is another important part of what's going on in this line of code: `>>> random.randint(1,100)`. You put the `random` module and the `randint` feature together with a dot.

The built-ins you saw earlier were referred to directly by their names. This way of referencing (called a *namespace*) turns out to be one honking great idea.

Attribute operator

I call the dot in `random.randint` the *attribute operator*. (Read why in Project 6.) I've seen other people call it that and have heard the process of referencing `random.randint` described as *namespace qualification*. I've tried to track down an official name for it, but haven't been successful. What would you call it?

If you always refer to these features by their names without identifying their modules, then you'd have trouble. What if you had two modules with a feature of the same name? It would be like no one having a family name. Python would have the same trouble if you didn't identify a feature by its module name and its feature name.

 This idea of referencing part B of object A through the structure A.B is something that you end up doing a lot as you get more experienced at Python.

Finish Your Guessing Game

It's time to finish off the guessing game. The final touches on the guessing game turn out to be pretty straightforward. At the start of the program you

- ✔ `import` the `random` module

- ✔ Make the computer guess a number using `random.randint()`

- ✔ Store the computer's number

When you add these changes to the code, you get this. The first three lines are new:

```
>>> import random
>>>
>>> computers_number = random.randint(1,100)
>>> prompt = 'What is your guess? '
>>> while True:
...       players_guess = raw_input(prompt)
...       if computers_number == int(players_guess):
...            print('Correct!')
...            break
...       elif computers_number > int(players_guess):
...            print('Too low')
...       else:
...            print('Too high')
...
What is your guess? 24
Too low
What is your guess? 86
Too low
What is your guess? 94
Too low
What is your guess? 98
Too high
What is your guess? 96
Too high
What is your guess? 95
Correct!
```

Zen of Python

```
>>> import this
```

Summary

This project covered:

✔ Getting input from a user by prompting for information.

✔ Python treating numbers and strings differently, and getting a number from a string (`int`) and a string from a number (`str`).

✔ Testing whether two things are equal.

✔ Python's operators, including tricky stuff about integer versus floating-point division and how to join strings together with +.

✔ Five keywords: `break`, `elif`, `else`, `if`, and `import`. (Only 21 to go.)

✔ Python code blocks, that you need to align their indent levels, and that each indent level should be four spaces.

✔ A couple of built-ins — `int` and `str`.

✔ How to import modules from the standard library.

✔ The `random` module and its `random.randint` feature.

✔ Another value — `False`. (One to go.)

Set Up Your Coding Environment

Project 3 was kind of brutal, huh? This project is quick and painless. You read about the IDLE Python development environment, which lets you save your code into a file. (No more retyping or cutting and pasting!)

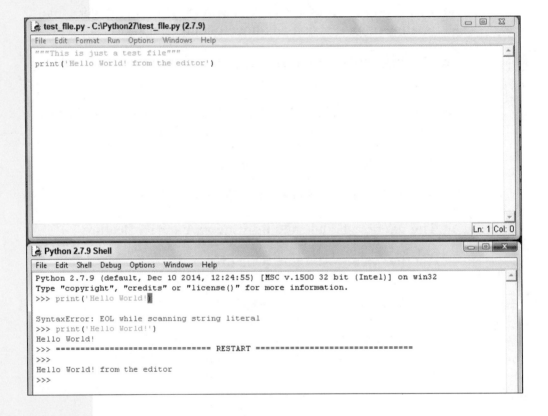

IDLE uses different colors to show the syntax of the Python code you're writing. It also has tools for commenting and indenting regions in and out. What's commenting? You read about that, too, along with some editing features that make coding easier.

Use the Default Development Environment

An *integrated development environment* is a kind of word processor for coding.

Never use a word processor for coding! Don't cut and paste from your word processor. Characters that work with Python get replaced with heinous ones that Python can't handle. For example, something like `message = 'Don't use Word!'` should create a string literal. If you copy and paste it from Word into Python, you get a syntax error on the first single quote. That's because ' isn't the same thing as '. These things — "" — are different from what Python uses: "".

The IDLE environment won't work if you're using Python on a tablet. Look at an app store for apps that give you a coding environment on your tablet.

Monty Python's BFF

Apparently IDLE stands for *Integrated Development Environment*. Did you know that the name of one of the comedians in the Monty Python comedy troupe was named Eric Idle? Another development environment for Python is called Eric.

Python comes with a code editor called IDLE. The editor has two main parts:

- The Shell window gives you the Python prompt shown in Figure 4-1.

- The Editor window lets you save and run your files.

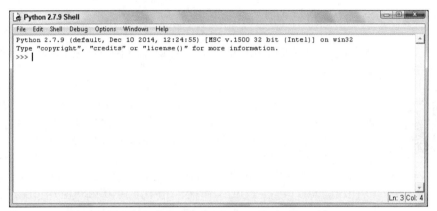

Figure 4-1: My IDLE's shrunken Shell window looks like this.

Start IDLE

In Project 1 you pin IDLE (Python GUI) to the top of your Start menu. It should still be up there.

1. Start IDLE by clicking the Windows Start menu.

   When you start IDLE, you should see the Shell window with the Python interactive prompt. (It's shown in Figure 4-1.) Yours may be a bit longer. I shrunk mine to keep from wasting paper.

   To open the IDLE Shell on Mac: Open a terminal and type IDLE at the prompt. The IDLE Shell window opens.

For the rest of your projects, start up IDLE and use IDLE's Shell window when you see the > > > prompts, or when I ask you to start a copy of Python I mean to start IDLE and use IDLE's Shell window.

2. Type the Hello World! program from Project 2 into the prompt.

You should get a pleasant surprise like the one in Figure 4-2.

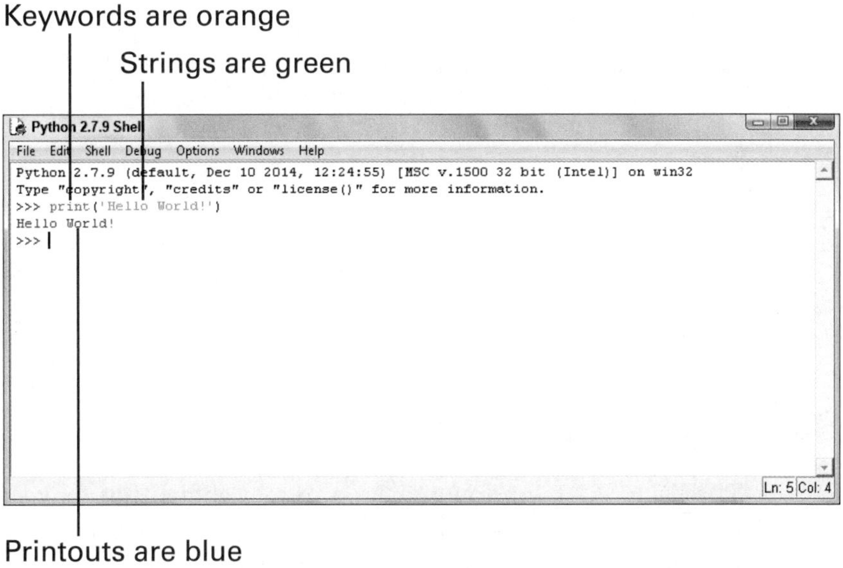

Keywords are orange

Strings are green

Printouts are blue

Figure 4-2: Syntax highlights put your code in different colors.

IDLE shows you all parts of the program, including Python's output, in different colors. IDLE gives different colors to keywords (like print), strings (like 'Hello World!'), and numbers. These color cues can be helpful when you're programming.

In Figure 4-3 the closing parenthesis is still green, not black. This means that Python still thinks it's part of a string literal. You know then that you have to put in a closing quote. What's more, when you press Enter, IDLE highlights the error.

In addition to the error notice that you get from the Python interpreter, IDLE gives you visual feedback about where it thinks there's a problem. Of course, IDLE isn't always right.

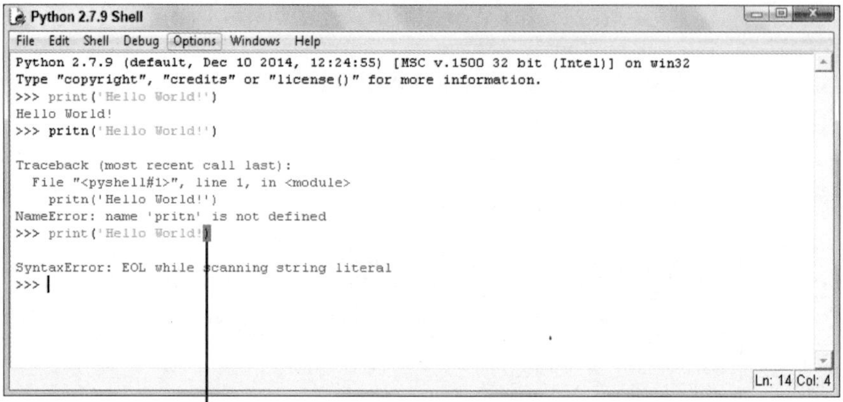

Python thinks the error is here

Figure 4-3: IDLE highlights your error.

Stash Some IDLE Tricks

The IDLE Shell window has a couple of tricks that make coding a little easier. Tab completion and command history are two good tricks.

Tab completion

Tab completion is using the Tab key to finish your typing for you. Try it out with these steps:

1. Start a new line in the Shell window.

2. Type p and press the Tab key. This is tab completion at work!

   A drop-down window appears, giving you different options. In Figure 4-4 you can see the window.

3. Press the arrow key to get to print in the drop-down window.

   The p that you typed changes to the word print.

4. Type ('Hello World!') and then press Enter.

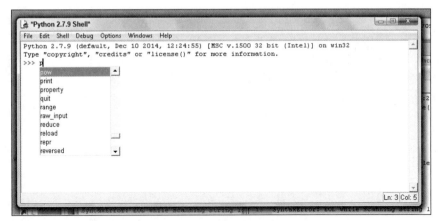

Figure 4-4: Press the Tab key to open this drop-down menu.

Keep typing to close the drop-down window; don't press Enter. If you press Enter while you're there, you'll muck up the completion. If typing is just too weird for you, press the Tab key twice to accept the highlighted selection. Weird, I know.

Tab completion also works with the names of variables that you've already created. Try this example:

1. Start a new line in the Shell window.

2. Type `this_is_a_long_variable_name = 0`.

3. Press Enter.

4. Type `thi` and press the Tab key.

   Yes, type only t, h, and i.

   The whole variable name should be typed out for you now. Only one variable matches the completion for *thi,* so you don't have to choose from a list.

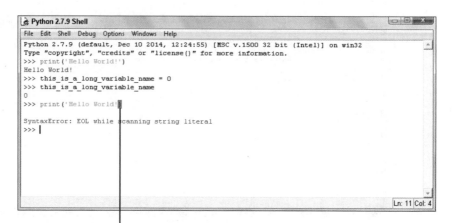

Oops. That's mistyped

Figure 4-5: Python's hissing about an error.

Command history

IDLE lets you go back and edit your mistakes using command history. To use command history, follow these steps:

1. Use the up arrow key to go back to the line you want to run again.

2. Press Enter.

   The code at the current command prompt is copied. If there's a code block (such as one associated with a conditional statement like `if`), then the whole code block is also copied.

3. Use the arrow, Backspace, and Delete keys to edit the line.

4. Press Enter to run the code.

Try it yourself:

1. Type `print('Hello World!)` at the prompt.

   Yes, just the one quote. The line is intentionally wrong.

2. Press Enter.

   Python complains about a syntax error, like you see in Figure 4-5.

3. Press the up arrow key until the cursor is back on the previous line.

   You should have to press it three times.

4. Press Enter.

   A copy of the code appears at the interpreter prompt. See the copied line in Figure 4-6.

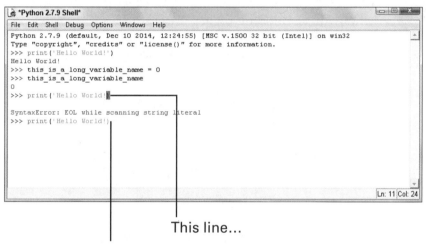

This line...

... has been copied here.
Edit and press Enter.

Figure 4-6: Command line history copies lines so you can fix errors.

5. Use the arrow keys to go to the end of the line.

6. Insert the closing quote and then press Enter.

Using command line history is often easier than retyping the whole line again. Missing quote marks, misspellings, and bad syntax are cases where it's good to use.

Use the IDLE Editor Window

IDLE's Editor window is where you'll spend most of your programming hours. The main thing about the Editor window is that you get to save your typing (unlike the Shell window). You can save your programs and run them without having to retype them every time. (Yay!)

Use the Shell window to test a single command or small sections of code. Use the Editor window to create, save, and edit your code when you're building bigger programs.

You can open an Editor window through the menu bar in the Shell window.

- ✐ In Windows, choose File ➪ New File. Or, type Ctrl+N in the Shell window.

- ✐ On a Mac, in the Shell window, choose File ➪ New Window. Or, select Cmd+N in the Shell window.

You get a clean, shiny new window.

This window doesn't have the interpreter prompt or the message telling you what version of Python you're using. That's because it's not for directly running your code. Rather, it's for creating and saving your code into a file which can be run and edited later.

Saving your code in a file makes life a lot easier for you, especially as your programs grow larger. However, you don't get the immediate feedback you do when using the Shell.

Try this:

1. Look at the window's title bar.

   Right now it's named Untitled.

2. Type `"""This is just a test file"""` and press Enter.

This is called a comment, and I explain it in a minute.

3. Check the title bar again.

It's now `*Untitled*`. The stars (asterisks, really, but who asterisked me?) mean that you have unsaved changes in the file.

4. Type `print('Hello World! from the editor')` and press Enter.

Unlike in the Shell window, nothing happens. Your Editor window should look like Figure 4-7.

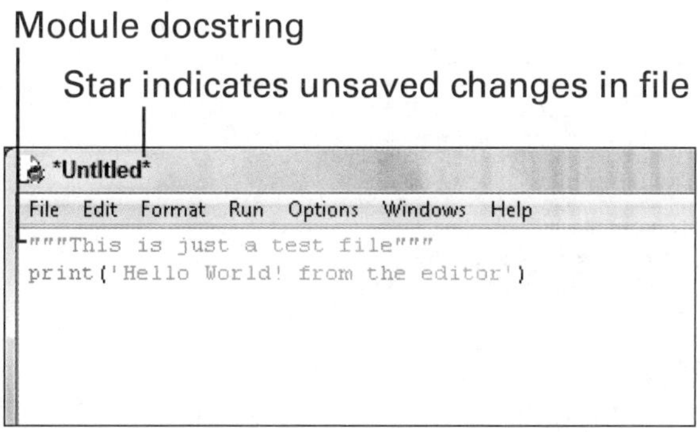

Module docstring

Star indicates unsaved changes in file

Figure 4-7: This program is in the IDLE Editor window.

5. Press the F5 key or choose Run ⇨ Run Module from the menu bar.

F5 is the function key at the top of your keyboard. When you take this step, IDLE says `Source Must Be Saved. OK to Save?`

6. Click OK on the dialog box.

A Save As dialog box opens in Windows.

7. Type `test_file.py` in the text box marked `File Name:`.

Remember to add `.py` to the end of the filename. IDLE won't do it for you.

Don't worry about the directory for now, just save it wherever IDLE wants.

8. Click the Save button.

If you get a dialog box like Figure 4-8, you've copied and pasted some quotes (typically from the program Word). If so, your code won't work. Go back through your code and replace quotes with real single or double quotes. (IDLE may or may not help with a syntax error in this case.)

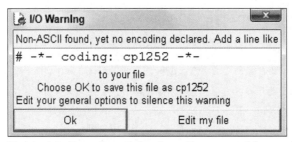

Figure 4-8: Encoding dialog box. If you see this, you've done something wrong.

When you click the Save button, IDLE saves your code into the file with the name you gave it (in this case, `test_file.py`). Then it runs that file and puts any output in the Shell window. Now the Shell window should look like Figure 4-9.

You can run the program again by pressing F5 as many times as you want. Each time the Shell window will restart. When the Shell restarts, you lose the values of any variables that you had earlier typed into the Shell. You also lose tab completion of those variable names.

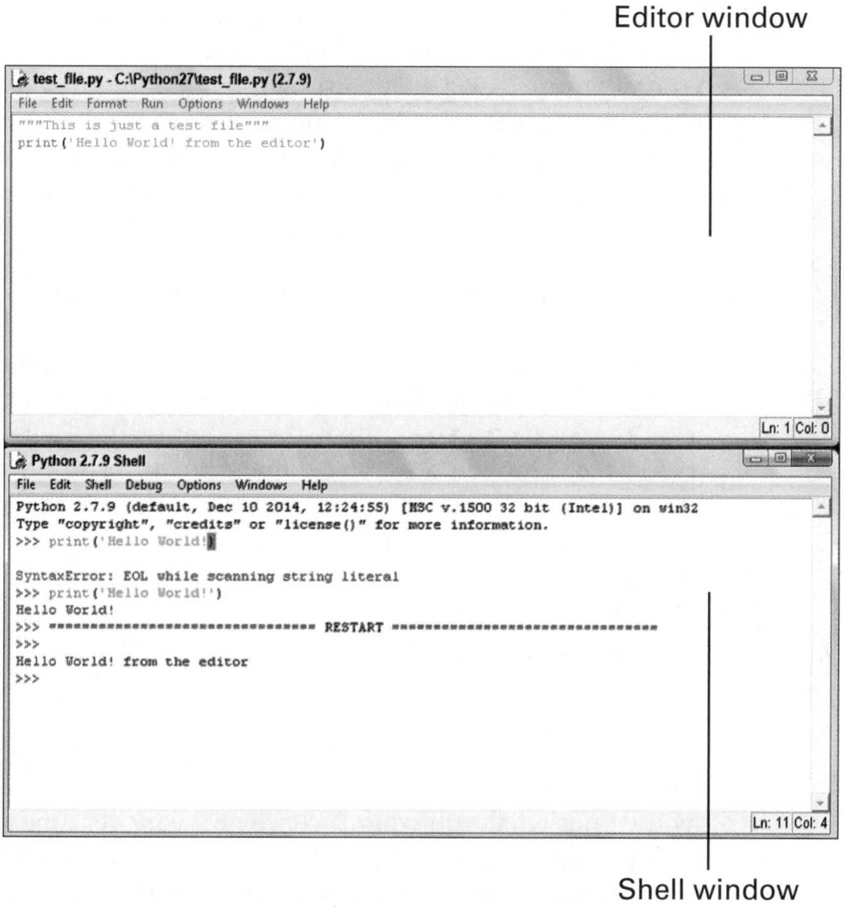

Editor window

Shell window

Figure 4-9: When you run a program in the Editor window (top), the Shell window restarts (bottom).

Write Comments in Your Files

The file you made in the previous section should look like this:

```
"""This is just a test file"""
print('Hello World! from the editor')
```

The first line here is called a *comment*. It looks like the string literals that you read about in Project 2 — because that's what it is. When Python sees a string literal in a file it ignores it! This is a good thing because you can communicate messages to your future self through the comments in the program text. In this case, you're telling yourself that this file is just a test file, so you shouldn't be too bummed if you mess up.

You have a lot of good reasons to write comments in your code:

- **As an explanation.** Whenever you create a new Python file, write a short explanation of what the code's supposed to do. Don't repeat what the code is doing. Summarize what the code is for. What do you want to achieve? So, in the code `a = a+1 # adding 1 to a` the comment is pointless because any fool can see that the code is adding 1 to a. You'd generally not include a comment here unless there was a reason that is not clear from the code. For example: `a = a+1 # Changing a causes the data to be refreshed in the next code block`.

- **As a memory aid.** When you're first writing your code you're very close to it. You're familiar with it. You understand why you've put what you've put where and why. As time goes by, you will forget why you put that piece of code somewhere. It's a lot easier to read a description than work it out later.

- **As a means of communication.** When you give your code to someone else, an English explanation of what the code does is even more important. Comments allow you to *collaborate* (work together) better with others. If you want to work as part of a programming team, you'd better have good comments in your code.

- **As a debugging aid.** If there's a problem with your code, someone will need to go in and fix it, and it may not be you. Again, having an English explanation of what's going on is a big help.

- **Because it's good for you.** Like vegetables, only tastier.

Insert Hash Comments

Technically, any string literal can be a comment — but it's better to use literals with triple double quotes `"""Like this comment"""`. (Comments are like the basketball player of code: the triple double!) You can also make a comment by using a hash mark: #.

When Python finds a hash, it ignores everything following the hash on the line. Hashes are usually for comments at the end of a line or short comments in the middle of code. They're faster than a string literal, since you're only typing one character. However, if you want to use hashes for a comment that runs a couple of lines, you have to type a new hash at the start of each line.

Here is an example of code with both types of comment:

```
"""This is just a test file"""

print('Hello World! from the editor') # Use # for comments too!
""" You usually use hashes at the end of a line
rather than for a block comment like this one.
"""
###############################################################
# Nevertheless you can still use hashes for block comments
# Especially if you want to have a specific visual effect
###############################################################
print('See that the comments were ignored?') # even this one
```

Hashtag octothorpe

What I called a hash mark is usually called a number sign or a pound sign. (To complicate matters, in the United Kingdom, a pound sign is what they use for their money and it looks like this: £). Programmers usually call this a *hash*. You're probably familiar with Twitter hashtags (so-called because they're a tag starting with a hash). A fancier term for the symbol is *octothorpe*. *Hashtag octothorpe* would presumably look like this: ##.

> ## Windows directory
>
> In the previous section you saved your file just wherever Python felt like putting it. It should have ended up in C:\python27. Just dumping your files any old place isn't a good practice. Other times I want you to save your files into a separate directory that you set up for your Python work. IDLE automatically looks in C:\python27 (unless you're on a Mac) when you ask it to do anything, and having some files in a different directory would've made life difficult.

The comments inside triple double quotes can go over as many lines as you like; make sure to end with triple double quotes, too. This hashed block is technically four separate comments on consecutive lines.

Save Your Shell Contents

You might have thought the end of Project 3 was annoying when you had to keep retyping more or less the same code to play the guessing game. Never fear! Now you can save your program into a file and run it from there.

You can choose File ➪ Save from IDLE's Shell window to save the contents of the interpreter window. The saved parts include the opening version number notice and the interactive session at the Shell, which means you can't run the file as a Python program later. You only save the Shell session if there's output in your Shell that you want to keep.

Comment Out Code

Often when you're running a program you'll want to skip a block of code for one reason or another. For example, you might have a problem in one part, but the program goes through another section before it gets there. That other part of the code might take too long to get through or make it tough to understand a problem. Or maybe you want to try a different approach, so you comment out the original code while you test the variation.

If you want to temporarily stop code from executing, don't delete the code from the file. A better approach is to *comment out* the code. Comment out code by putting a hash in front of each line of code.

IDLE lets you comment out many lines at once. Here's how:

1. **Start with some code. Oh, here's one I prepared earlier:**

   ```
   """This is a file to use when demonstrating
   how to comment out a code block. """

   # this section is holding us up for some reason

   print('Imagine that instead of these print statements,')
   print('there is instead some code which, if it runs')
   print('will complicate the process of debugging some later piece')
   print('of code. ')

   # This is the later section which needs to be debugged

   print('Hello World! ')
   # imagine there's more program below as well
   ```

2. **Select the lines to comment out.**

   Click and drag with your mouse to select the code, or press Shift while using your arrow keys. See the highlighted code in Figure 4-10.

3. **Choose Format ➪ Comment Out Region.**

   Alt+3 and Alt-O also work. After you do that, the selected code should have hash marks in front of it. You can see the results in Figure 4-11.

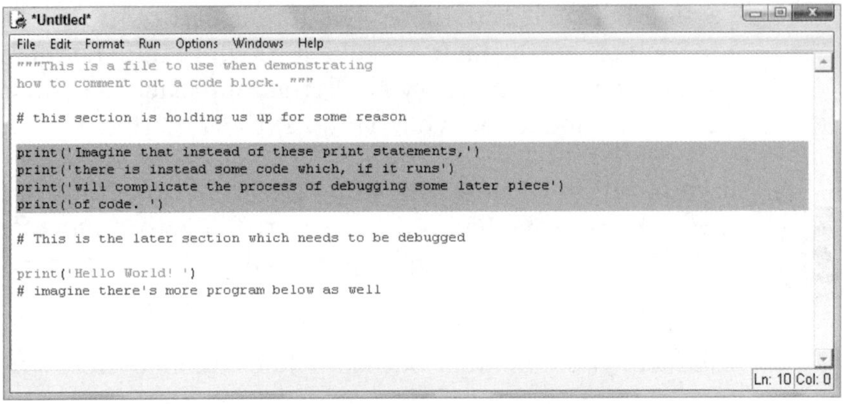

Figure 4-10: Select the code that you want commented out.

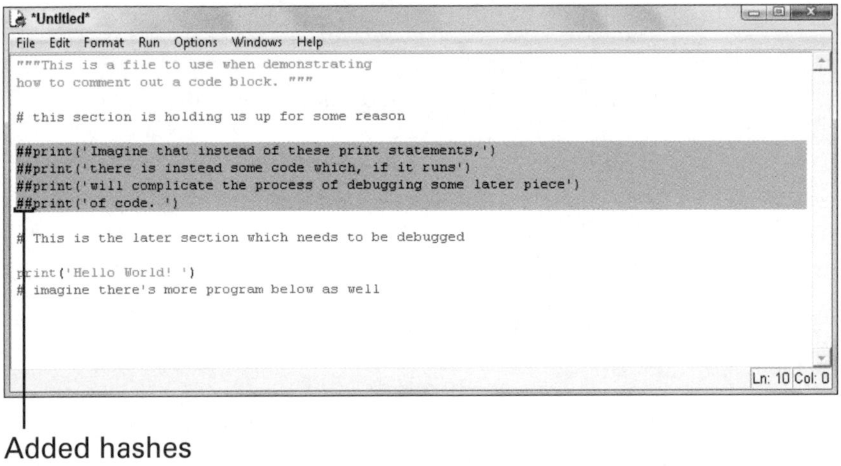

Added hashes

Figure 4-11: Hashes are added after you comment out code.

Now when you run the code, the commented-out sections are skipped. Maybe you found the problem and debugged the block. You can *reinstate* (convert it from a comment to code) commented-out code with these steps:

1. Select the lines to be reinstated.

2. Choose Format ⇨ Uncomment Region.

   Alt+4 and Alt-O, N also work. Your code is restored to normal.

Indent and Dedent Your Code

You're going to have to change the number of spaces in front of one or more lines of code. It's common in programming. Moving them in is *indenting*. Moving them out is *dedenting* (or *deindenting*).

For example, if you want to move a print statement from the main part of the program into the code block of a loop, you need to indent it. To move it out of the code block of a loop, you need to deindent it. IDLE has tools to indent and dedent code blocks.

Try those -denting tools:

1. Start with some code.

   Here's some:

   ```
   """This is just a test file"""
   DEBUG = True
   print('Hello World! from the editor') # Use # for comments too!
   """ You usually use hashes at the end of a line
   rather than for a block comment like this one.
   """
   ################################################################
   # Nevertheless you can still use hashes for block comments
   # Especially if you want to have a specific visual effect
   ################################################################

   if DEBUG:
       print('I think I need another print statement.')

       print('See that the comments were ignored?') # even this one
   ```

2. Select the lines to indent.

   Click and drag with your mouse to select the code (the last print statement), or press Shift while using your arrow keys.

3. Choose Format ⇨ Indent Region.

   Ctrl+] also works.

4. Make sure the code's indented into a valid code block.

Indentation is meaningful to Python. You'll get a syntax error if you have the wrong level of indent.

It's best to use four spaces of indent for each code block level. If you use another number of spaces (2, 6, 8), that's fine. The important thing is that all the code in the code block must have the same number of spaces.

To go the other way, select the code and choose File ⇨ Dedent Region (or press Ctrl+[).

Summary

In this project you

- ✔ Started and stopped IDLE.

- ✔ Checked out IDLE's Shell window and Editor window.

- ✔ Included comments in your code.

- ✔ Commented out code, and commented it back in.

- ✔ Indented and dedented (deindented) a code block.

A Better Guessing Game

In this project you read about one of the main parts of programming — functions. You take that knowledge and convert your Project 3 guessing game from Project 3 so that it uses functions, which will allow you to structure the program in a more easily understood way.

```
                        guess_game_fun.py - /data-current/dummies book/code_folder/guess_game_fun.py

File  Edit  Format  Run  Options  Windows  Help

"""guess_game_fun
Guess Game with a Fun ction
In this project the guess game is recast using a function"""

import random

PROMPT = 'What is your guess? '

# New constants
QUIT = -1
QUIT_TEXT = 'q'
QUIT_MESSAGE = 'Thank you for playing'
CONFIRM_QUIT_MESSAGE = 'Are you sure you want to quit (Y/n)? '

# New confirm_quit function
def confirm_quit():
    """Ask user to confirm that they want to quit
    default to yes
    Return True (yes, quit) or False (no, don't quit) """
    spam = raw_input(CONFIRM_QUIT_MESSAGE)
    if spam == 'n':
        return False
    else:
        return True

def do_guess_round():
    """Choose a random number, ask the user for a guess
    check whether the guess is true
    and repeat until the user is correct"""
    computers_number = random.randint(1,100)
    number_of_guesses = 0
    while True:
        players_guess = raw_input(PROMPT)
        # new if clause to test against quit
        if players_guess == QUIT_TEXT:
            if confirm_quit():
                return QUIT
            else:
                continue # that is, do next round of loop
        number_of_guesses = number_of_guesses+1
        if computers_number == int(players_guess):
            print('Correct!')
            return number_of_guesses
        elif computers_number > int(players_guess):
            print('Too low')

                                                                                Ln: 1 Col: 0
```

As you work through this project, you'll see how to communicate to and from a function, as well as the transdimensional nature of variables. You also put together a function to confirm that the user wants to quit a program. You can reuse this function in your future projects. Reducing, recycling, and reusing — it's all coming together here.

Handle Your Functions

Functions are a simple way to group together actions. With them you can do some groups of actions repeatedly without having to retype all the code. You save typing, and it's easier to think about how to structure your program and to update it.

In Project 3, you had to retype the guessing game each time you wanted to run it — boring. You can avoid that by using what you read about in Project 4 — save the code to a file and run the file repeatedly. Or you can wrap all the code in a `while` clause.

One problem with these approaches: They don't let you reuse code in other circumstances. Besides comments, which get messy as programs get larger, you have no obvious way to tell what part of the code does what.

Think of when your parents tell you to get ready for school. They might say, "Get up, get dressed, have some breakfast, put your homework in your bag, put your lunch in your bag, brush your teeth." When they say, "Get ready for school," they're wrapping all those separate activities into one thing, like a `get_ready` function. They're also moving from the particular (detailed instructions on what to do and how to do it) to the general (getting ready). This is called *abstraction.*

Whenever you move from thinking less about details, you're being more *abstract* (or you've accidentally gone to sleep). When you abstract things, you can plan with general concepts but tackle each separate task. Plan your own programs using functions as your level of abstraction, then tackle what each function does separately. Divide, then conquer!

Functions let you explain what does what, and functions let you reuse your code.

To use a function, you must

✔ Define the function itself

✔ *Invoke,* or call, the function

Here's a simple example that reworks your Hello World! program using a function. Open IDLE and type this in the Shell window:

```
>>> def print_hello_world():
        """Hello World as a function"""
        print('Hello World!')
```

Remember to press Enter twice to return to the command prompt.

It doesn't *do* anything. A bit pointless? Sort of. You're defining the function (using the `def` keyword). Now, you must call the function to make it run:

```
>>> print_hello_world()
Hello World!
```

As you can see from Figure 5-1, Python will *call* the function if you write the function's name followed by parentheses. This means that as Python flows through your program, when it reaches the function call it continues at the function definition and runs through the code in that function's code block.

A function's *code block* is the line following the `def` statement up to (but not including) the next line that's indented the same as the `def` statement. You can see some code blocks pointed out in Figure 5-2.

Comment line; no action

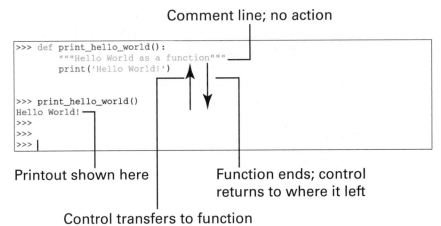

Printout shown here

Control transfers to function

Function ends; control returns to where it left

Figure 5-1: Program flows into and out of the function.

`confirm_quit` code block

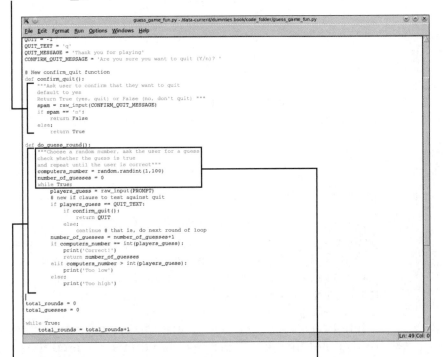

`do_guess_round` code block

First level indented four spaces

Figure 5-2: The do_guess_round code block holds the while loop.

When the Python reaches the end of the function, it skips back to the spot where the call occurred (back there with the parentheses).

Including the parentheses with the function call is important. If you leave them out Python doesn't call the function. Instead it tells you about the function:

```
>>> print_hello_world
<function print_hello_world at 0x7f8dd8043b90>
```

Here it's telling you that `print_hello_world` is a function, and that its name is `print_hello_world`. The bit at the end is where in memory the Python keeps the function.

Naming Functions

The rules for naming a function are a lot like rules for naming a variable:

✔ They must start with a letter or an underscore: _.

✔ They should be lowercase.

✔ They can have numbers.

✔ They can be any length (within reason), but keep them short.

✔ They can't be the same as a Python keyword. They can have the same name as an existing function (including a built-in), but avoid this for now.

The function `print_hello_world` is very basic. It only does one thing. It can't respond to different circumstances because no information is passing into the function when you call it.

This is fine if you need to do the same thing all the time. Functions are even more powerful, though, because you can communicate with them and they can do different things depending on the information. You could change this function and send it different messages to print.

Functions are extremely useful and powerful tools in your programming toolbox because they allow you to separate your program into meaningful blocks. All the built-ins in Python are functions, as is everything in the standard library.

Add Function Help Text

Project 4 explains comments and how to include them in a program to explain *what* the program's doing or *why* it's doing what it's doing.

Functions have a special kind of comment, called a *docstring*. The main purpose of a docstring is to explain (possibly to your future self) what the function's supposed to do. This means that someone looking through your code (most likely you) will understand what the function is doing without having to figure out the code itself (which may not be obvious).

To create a docstring, add a string literal enclosed in triple double quotes as the first line of the function's code block, like this:

```
>>> def test_function():
        """Just a function stub to illustrate some basic things about
    docstrings. Add a docstring as a string literal at the start of the
    function code block. Use triple double quotes."""
        pass
```

The Python style guide for docstrings is called PEP257 (the Python people can be a little unromantic sometimes) and it goes on forever! How much could you possibly say about docstrings? Lots, apparently. The next time you get bored playing computer games, spend some time going through PEP257 in detail. I dare you.

Until then, take away these key bits about docstrings:

✔ The docstring should be *delimited* (surrounded) by triple double quotes, like this: `"""This is a docstring"""`. Put three double quotes at the start of the string and three at the end of the string. Don't put them on every line.

✔ The docstring should explain what the function is supposed to do. Your parents' get_ready function might have the docstring "Get each kid ready for school". It explains what it's achieving, not how it's achieving it.

✔ The docstring should be written using sentences. In English! (Or whatever your native language is.)

✔ Don't worry if you can't explain everything about the function. Write what you want the function to do; don't write *how* it does it. You can change docstrings later as you write the function.

Ideally, every function has a docstring. However, whether you should write a docstring for a function depends on how long you'll use the program and how complicated the function is.

Use a string literal rather than a hash comment for a docstring. Some tools automatically look for string literals. In fact, now you can automagically use Python's help for this function, even though you've only just defined it:

```
>>> help(test_function)
>>> Help on function test_function in module __main__:

test_function()
    Just a function stub to illustrate some basic things
    about docstrings. Add a docstring as a string literal
    at the start of the function code block. Use triple
    double quotes.
```

You might find using docstrings a bit boring or pointless. Fight that feeling! Including docstrings is an excellent habit to get into, particularly if you want to program for a living. Believe me, if they hire you, Google will expect you to comply with PEP8.

> # Automagic
>
> If your program does something automatically for you and you're really surprised that it can be done so easily, it's done it *automagically* for you.

There are tools that pull out these docstrings. If you include docstrings for all your functions, you have a quick way to put together initial documentation for your program. It'll save you time later.

Make a Function Stub

If you know that you're going to need a function but aren't sure on the details, you can use the `pass` keyword and leave the code block to be filled in later. In the following code, you know you need to solve world hunger in the function, but aren't quite sure how. Make a function placeholder with `pass` and figure out the details later:

```
>>> def solve_world_hunger():
        pass
```

An empty function like this — a *stub* — lets you define the function (it will fail if there's no code block) but work out the details later. It's mainly a placeholder to help you organize your thoughts.

If you include a docstring, then you don't need the `pass` statement. It's probably better if you include the docstring. If you can't think of what the docstring should be, that's a sign that you don't need that function at all. (Perhaps it's already covered by other functions you've written.)

```
>>> def solve_world_hunger():
        """This is a function that I will write later.
        It will automatically feed the world's starving masses"""
```

Get to know `main`

It's easy to talk about the code in a function. I can talk about the `solve_world_hunger` code and it's clear that I'm talking about the code in the function's code block. How do I draw your attention to code that isn't part of a function? The top level of the program or module — all the code at the first indent level and that doesn't define something else — is called `main`. (Why? I don't know. I guess this is a throwback to other programming languages which expected a function called `main` as their entry point.)

Assume you have a program like this:

```
""" A teeny tiny program to demonstrate main"""

def test_function():
    """ Just a nothing function. Ignore it"""

test_function()
```

The code in the `test_function` code block is identified by its function name — `test_function`. The call to `test_function()` occurs in `main`. So what? Now you'll know what I mean when I talk about `main` in the coming pages.

Rework Your Guessing Game

By the time you got to the end of Project 3, your program looked something like this. I ditched the >>> prompts.

```
import random

computers_number = random.randint(1,100)
prompt = 'What is your guess? '
```

```
while True:
    players_guess = raw_input(prompt)
    if computers_number == int(players_guess):
        print('Correct!')
        break
    elif computers_number > int(players_guess):
        print('Too low')
    else:
        print('Too high')
```

It's pretty simple to make all this code (other than the `import`) into a function. Do the following:

1. Create a new file in IDLE.

   Check back in Project 4 if you need to.

2. Add a module docstring at the start of the file to explain what the program does.

   Use triple double quotes at the beginning and end of the docstring.

3. Save the file, call it `guess_game_fun.py`.

4. Re-type the code from Project 3.

   Now you're going to update it to make use of a function.

5. Create a function named `do_guess_round`.

6. Create a function stub for `do_guess_round`.

7. Add a docstring for the function.

   Use triple double quotes at the beginning and end of the docstring.

8. Move the `while` loop copied from Project 3 to the `do_guess_round` function.

9. Indent the code to make it part of the function's code block. Use IDLE's Format ⇨ Indent Region or Ctrl+].

10. Add a line to call the do_guess_round function.

```
do_guess_round()
```

11. Save the file.

When you save the file, it should highlight any code that it thinks has syntax errors. If you get an error, check your spelling and make sure both beginning and ending quote marks are there.

12. Press F5 or choose Run ⇨ Run Module from the menu.

See if the guess game works like it did in Project 3. I got this.

Listing 5-2

```
"""guess_game_fun
Guess Game with a Function
In this project the guess game is recast using a function"""

import random

computers_number = random.randint(1,100)
PROMPT = 'What is your guess? '

def do_guess_round():
    """Choose a random number, ask the user for a guess
    check whether the guess is true
    and repeat until the user is correct"""
    while True:
        players_guess = raw_input(PROMPT)
        if computers_number == int(players_guess):
            print('Correct!')
            break
```

```
        elif computers_number > int(players_guess):
            print('Too low')
        else:
            print('Too high')

do_guess_round()
```

Listing 5-2 has a couple more changes in it. I changed the name prompt to PROMPT. It's a convention (kind of a rule) to store values that you don't intend to change in a "variable" (in quotes, because it's not actually a variable) with a name written in ALL_CAPS. Since the prompt is supposed to be the same all the time, I changed its name to be in all caps.

A variable that isn't supposed to vary is a *constant*. (You might also see the word *static* used for constants.) Place all constants at the start of your file; don't scatter them throughout the code.

In a Python file, a function's definition must occur before the first call to that function.

Find a Logic Problem

But wait! The code in the previous section has a problem. It'll become obvious when you try putting the question rounds (from the time the computer asks the user to guess the number until the user guesses correctly is one round of questions) inside a loop.

Change do_guess_round() at the end of the program to this:

```
while True:
    do_guess_round()
```

Save and run the code by pressing F5 from the Editor window:

```
>>> =================================== RESTART
==============================
>>>
```

```
What is your guess? 67
Too low
What is your guess? 87
Too low
What is your guess? 97
Too low
What is your guess? 99
Too low
What is your guess? 100
Correct!
What is your guess? 10
Too low
What is your guess? 56
Too low
What is your guess? 99
Too low
What is your guess? 100
Correct!
What is your guess? 50
Too low
What is your guess? 99
Too low
What is your guess? 100
Correct!
What is your guess? 100
Correct!
What is your guess? 100
Correct!
What is your guess?
```

Well shoot. The program has two problems:

✔ Every time the game restarts, the computer's answer is exactly the same (in this case, 100). That's not how the game should run! The computer should choose a different number for each round.

Can you work out why? Because the number is the same each time, it's probably an issue with how it's chosen or how it's stored. Think about the path Python follows when it flows through this code and where the number choice occurs in relation to this flow. I'll tell you what's up in a couple of paragraphs.

✔ You can't tell when a question round has ended and when a new question round has begun.

Solve the Logic Problem

The program keeps guessing the same number because of an issue with the location of the `random.randint()` function. The program goes through these steps when you run the program:

1. Executes the import.

2. Chooses a random number.

3. Assigns a value to `PROMPT`.

4. Defines a function but doesn't execute it yet.

5. Starts a loop.

6. Repeatedly calls the function from inside the loop. It keeps jumping to the code in Step 4, without going to Step 2 to choose a new random number.

When it calls the function, the random number isn't chosen again. The same number is used each time. You can fix it by putting the code choosing the number *inside* the function. You can separate the rounds by adding `print` statements to clarify when a new round has begun. A line that prints the value of the computer's guess helps you understand what's happening in the program.

Here's a new version with these problems fixed:

```
"""guess_game_fun
Guess Game with a Function
In this project the guess game is recast using a function"""


import random


computers_number = random.randint(1,100)
PROMPT = 'What is your guess? '


def do_guess_round():
    """Choose a random number, ask the user for a guess
    check whether the guess is true
    and repeat until the user is correct"""
    computers_number = random.randint(1,100)  # Added
    while True:
        players_guess = raw_input(PROMPT)
        if computers_number == int(players_guess):
            print('Correct!')
            break
        elif computers_number > int(players_guess):
            print('Too low')
        else:
            print('Too high')


while True:
    # Print statements added:
    print("Starting a new Round!")
    print("The computer's number should be "+str(computers_number))
    print("Let the guessing begin!!!")
    do_guess_round()
    print("") # blank line
```

I added two new parts shown with comments. The first addition makes the computer think up a number each time the function is called. The second adds some `print` statements to indicate when a new round of questioning has started.

Notice Double Use of `computers_number`

Adding a new line choosing a random number inside the function solves the logic problem. If that's all you were going to do, you'd delete the first reference to `computers_number`. You don't delete it because I want you to notice two things in the next readout:

- First, the program seems to be working as if there are two variables named `computers_number`. You can tell this because even though you print the number (`print("The computer's number should be "+str(computers_number))`), the value of the correct guess is different.

- Second, even though new values keep getting assigned to a variable named `computers_number` inside the function, those assignments don't change the value outside the function.

Run your own copy now (press Ctrl+C to quit) to see it happen. In my printout below, each time the function was called `computers_number` was 50. However, each time I guessed the answer correctly `computers_number` was something else (first 73, then 17).

```
Starting a new Round!
The computer's number should be 50
Let the guessing begin!!!
What is your guess? 50
Too low
What is your guess? 75
Too high
What is your guess? 63
Too low
What is your guess? 68
Too low
What is your guess? 72
Too low
What is your guess? 73
Correct!
```

```
Starting a new Round!
The computer's number should be 50
Let the guessing begin!!!
What is your guess? 50
Too high
What is your guess? 25
Too high
What is your guess? 12
Too low
What is your guess? 18
Too high
What is your guess? 15
Too low
What is your guess? 16
Too low
What is your guess? 17
Correct!

Starting a new Round!
The computer's number should be 50
Let the guessing begin!!!
What is your guess?
```

Understand How Scope Works

There's a lot of deep stuff going on in this bit of code. You're seeing an example of a variable's scope. A variable's *scope* is that part of the program where Python thinks the variable's name has a meaning. This gets tricky (and wonderful) because the same name can exist in many different places in a program. The variable's scope allows Python to make sense of which meaning you're using for a given name.

In the earlier code, the name `computers_number` is used more than once. There's one inside the function `do_guess_round` and one defined in `main`, but never the twain shall meet. It's like they're in different dimensions. What happens to one in one dimension doesn't happen to the other. In fact, each time the function `do_guess_round` is called, the variable is a different variable (but has the same name)! The program doesn't remember the value it had the last time the function was called.

 Variables that you define inside a function (including variables that get their values by having them passed as arguments) are called *local variables*. This means that when you're choosing the name of a variable to use inside your function, you don't need to remember the names of all the other variables you've ever used.

But it gets weirder! If variables live in different dimensions based on the function they're in, how come `computers_number` wasn't inside the function in Listing 5-2? How did the function "see" the variable to use that value?

When Python sees a reference to the value of a variable name, it looks in the current function to find whether that variable is assigned a value at any point in that function. If it can't find a variable of that name in the function, it looks up to `main` to see if there is a variable of that name. If there is, Python uses that variable's value.

The reverse isn't true, though. If you ask Python to name a variable by storing a value in it, Python creates a new variable within the function. Python can reach through the programming dimensions to get a value from the main part of the program, but (ordinarily) it can't change what's stored in `main`'s variables.

The following example names a variable `A` in `main` and defines three functions — `test1`, `test2`, and `test3`. Each of these test functions tries to print a variable called `A`. Before you look at the printout here, try to work out what `test1`, `test2`, and `test3` will print.

```
""" locals.py
examples of local variables"""
```

```
A = 'This is the text message from main'

def test1():
    print('In test1.')
    print(A)
    print('Leaving test1.')

def test2():
    print('In test2.')
    A = "This is test2's text message."
    print(A)
    print('Leaving test2.')

def test3():
    print('In test3.')
    print(A)
    A = "This is test3's text message."
    print('Leaving test3')

test1()
print('Back in main')
print(A)
test2()
print('Back in main')
print(A)
test3()
```

This gives the output shown in Figure 5-3.

In the function `test1`, Python reaches back through the dimensions to the main part of the program to get the value of A. It doesn't change the value. In `test2`, Python assigns a value to A and prints it. After Python returns from the function, the value of A in `main` is unchanged.

Why does `test3` fail completely? The only difference between `test2` and `test3` is the fact that a value is assigned to A before the `print` statement in `test2`, but after it in `test3`. In both the functions a value is assigned to A inside the function, so Python knows that there is (or will be) a variable called A in the function's own dimension (called its *scope*). As such, Python refuses to reach outside the function to get a value from main. In test3 Python needs a value for A. Python knows that A will be assigned a value somewhere in test3, which makes it a local variable. Python refuses to get a value for it from main, even though it doesn't yet have a value in test3. It can't get a value from within test3 because the A in test3 hasn't been given a value by the time Python reaches the print statement.

Value of A taken from test2's variable A

Value of A taken from Main

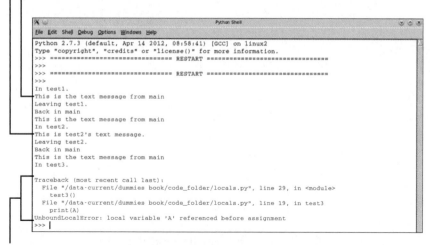

```
Python Shell
File Edit Shell Debug Options Windows Help
Python 2.7.3 (default, Apr 14 2012, 08:58:41) [GCC] on linux2
Type "copyright", "credits" or "license()" for more information.
>>> ================================ RESTART ================================
>>>
>>> ================================ RESTART ================================
>>>
In test1.
This is the text message from main
Leaving test1.
Back in main
This is the text message from main
In test2.
This is test2's text message.
Leaving test2.
Back in main
This is the text message from main
In test3.
Traceback (most recent call last):
  File "/data-current/dummies book/code_folder/locals.py", line 29, in <module>
    test3()
  File "/data-current/dummies book/code_folder/locals.py", line 19, in test3
    print(A)
UnboundLocalError: local variable 'A' referenced before assignment
>>>
```

Python wants to use test3's A, but it hasn't been assigned a value

Figure 5-3: The value for a variable depends on its scope.

Communicate with Your Function

So far, there's no communication between a function and main. No information is passed from main to the function, nor from a function back to main. They'd work better as a team. Fortunately,

Python knows how to communicate with a function and how a function can communicate back to what has called it. You'll do both in the next sections.

Send Information to a Function

You already have one, somewhat limited, form of sending information to a function — using a variable in the main part of the program when there's no variable of the same name within the function *and* no value is assigned to the variable inside the function. In that case, the function can receive the value of the variable.

Except in the case of constants (which is totally fine), this way of communicating information to a function is bad. Don't do it!

Python has a better way of communicating data to a function. In fact, functions are designed to receive data different ways. To have a function receive data, you must:

1. Decide how many separate pieces of information that the function is to receive. There's a limit, but it's more than you'll ever need.

2. For each piece, choose a name for a variable to receive the information.

3. List each variable name in the definition of the function.

The spaces are right for an argument

```
>>> def add_one(a_number):
        print(a_number)

>>> add_one(1)
1
>>> add_one(4)
4
```

Argument

Figure 5-4: You're assigning values to arguments by position.

Right room for an argument

The Monty Python troupe has a skit where a person tries to hire someone to have an argument with them. The first person argues that simply contradicting the other person doesn't qualify as an argument (arguing, in effect, that he's not getting the argument he paid for). The other person contradicts him, effectively arguing that just saying "No, it isn't" over and over is, in fact, an argument.

Each variable that's listed in parentheses in a function's definition is called an *argument*.

Fire up the Python interpreter and try the code in Figure 5-4.

The function's name is a little misleading in Figure 5-4, since it doesn't add one (I get to that later). What it does show is that the function receives the number that's been given to it. When add_one(1) starts, a local variable called a_number is created, then the value 1 is stored in a_number. On the next line, the function prints that value (because it's stored in the variable called a_number). That's the end of the function's code block, so execution stops there and continues from the point where the function was called. Put arguments in parentheses to pass them.

If the function has been defined to need an argument, you must pass a value to it, or it will get upset:

```
>>> add_one()

Traceback (most recent call last):
  File "<pyshell#7>", line 1, in <module>
    add_one()
TypeError: add_one() takes exactly 1 argument (0 given)
```

This telling you that the add_one function requires one value to be passed to it (called an *argument*), but that you haven't actually passed it a value like you're supposed to.

You can have more than one argument for a function, as long as you provide a value for each of those arguments. The following code has two arguments — a and b. When it's called, the numbers 1 and 2 are passed to the function and assigned to a and b, in that order. Put a comma between the arguments.

```
>>> def print_two_numbers(a,b):
        print(a,b)

>>> print_two_numbers(1,2)
(1, 2)
```

You can pass in more than one value if the function has been designed to receive them. Values are assigned to variables in the order the variables are listed: *positional arguments*. In Figure 5-5, the values 1 and 2 are assigned to the variables b and a, in order, because this is how they're listed in the function definition.

```
>>> def print_two_numbers(b,a):
        print("a= "+str(a)+", b='+str(b))

>>> print_two_numbers(1,2)
a= 2, b=1
```

Figure 5-5: Values are assigned to arguments according to where they are in the function's definition.

Give Some Arguments a Default Value

Positional arguments are passed to a function by their position in the list of arguments. You also can define arguments to have a default value. These are *keyword arguments*.

If you specify a default value for an argument, then you don't need to specify a value for that argument when you call the function. If you don't specify a value, the relevant variable gets its default value.

You make an argument have a default value by assigning the value in the function's definition.

Here is an example where the variable `display` is assigned a default value of `True` by the code `display=True`:

```
>>> def add_one(a,b,display=True):
        if display:
            print("a= "+str(a))
            print("b= "+str(b))

>>> add_one(1,2)
a= 1
b= 2
>>> add_one(1,2,False)
>>>
```

Here `display` is an argument with a default value. Its default value is `True`. In the line `add_one(1,2)`, no value was specified for this variable (the two values passed were used up on the variables `a` and `b`), so it took the value `True` and the two lines of the printout occurred.

In the line `add_one(1,2,False)`, a value (`False`) is specified for the variable `display`. Because of that, it is assigned that value. The condition `if display:` isn't satisfied, so nothing is printed.

List keyword arguments *after* positional arguments in the function's definition:

```
>>> def add_one(display=True,a,b):
        pass
SyntaxError: non-default argument follows default argument
```

You can have multiple default arguments in a function. They're assigned to the keyword variables in the order they're listed. This might cause a problem if you want to accept the default value for earlier but not later keyword arguments. If you leave them out, the values won't line up with the right arguments.

Python has a special syntax when there are multiple default arguments. Within the call to the function, you assign a value to the variable. In the following example, this is `include_pumpkin=False, display=False`. If you've explicitly given them a value, you can provide the default arguments in any order.

```
>>> def add_one(a,b,include_pumpkin=False,display=False):
        filler = " "
        if include_pumpkin:
            filler = " pumpkin! "
        if display:
            print(str(a)+filler+str(b))

>>> add_one(1,2,True)
>>> # True being sent to include_pumpkin
>>> # but display still False so nothing is printed
>>> add_one(1,2,True,True)  # True being sent to both
1 pumpkin! 2
>>> add_one(1,2,display=True,include_pumpkin=True)
1 pumpkin! 2
>>> add_one(1,2,display=True,include_pumpkin=False)
1 2
```

In the call `add_one(1,2,display=True,include_pumpkin=True)`, you're specifying the values for the keyword arguments. You can specify keyword arguments in any order (unlike positional arguments, where the order is important) if you use the syntax `<variable name>= value`. Replace `variable name` with the actual variable name and `value` with, you know, the actual value.

In this example, the variables `display` and `include_pumpkin` have been specified in reverse order listed in the function's definition. In the last example, `add_one(1,2,display=True, include_pumpkin=False)`, the keyword argument `include_pumpkin` is explicitly given a value of `False`. This was unnecessary, since it defaults to `False` anyway.

Communicate from the Function

You now know that the main part of a program can communicate to a function. It can do so through passing arguments or by referencing a variable name that isn't also defined within the function (usually only for constants).

What you don't know is how a function can communicate back to the main part of the program, or with another function that has called it. Fortunately, Python can communicate with the part of the program that called it. It uses the keyword `return`.

Check this out:

```
>>> def add_one(a_number):
        return a_number+1
```

In this code snippet, `add_one` is now New and Improved! With Added 1! This function takes an argument called `a_number` and *returns* the value of `a_number` plus 1. It does this by using `return`.

Call the function and see how it works:

```
>>> add_one(4)
5
```

In the first (and only) line of the function's code block, it looks up the value (4) it has stored in `a_number`, adds 1 to it to give 5, then it returns the value 5 to the part of the program that called the function. At this point the function stops running and execution continues from the point at which the function was called.

You can keep the value returned by the function the same way you can store any other value — by assigning it to a variable. This example has a variable named `retval`:

```
>>> retval= add_one(4)
>>> retval
5
```

All functions return a value, even when you don't include a `return` statement. The `print_hello_world` function doesn't use the `return` statement. What do you think it returns?

```
>>> def print_hello_world():
        """Hello World as a function"""
        print('Hello World!')
```

Python's compilation

When Python runs any program, the first thing it does is convert the human-readable code into something that can run on the machine. It always reads through your whole code at least once before it starts executing. This is how it had a problem in the `test3` function.

```
>>> retval = print_hello_world()
Hello World!
>>> print(retval)
None
```

Even though the function doesn't explicitly return any value, the variable `retval` now has a value — None. It's like asking what the return value is and Python says, "There was none." You're never going to want to do this on purpose, but from time to time you'll get weird program behavior because you've expected a return value when there isn't one. You need to know this for your debugging skills (or skillz). I show you an example that gets me all the time in Project 6.

Add a Score

From the previous sections you know how to:

✔ Use a function's arguments to send information to that function.

✔ Send information from a function to that part of the program that called that function using the `return` statement.

Now it's time to spruce up your game a little by adding a score and an easier way to quit. You can't expect your user to know about Ctrl+C.

The program will be changed so that it keeps track of

✔ The number of rounds the user has played

✔ The total number of guesses made (from which the average number of guesses can be calculated)

You can add these features to your guess_game_fun.py code by making these changes to the code at Listing 5-2.

Tracking rounds:

1. Add a variable called total_rounds to the main.

2. Increment (increase by 1) total_rounds in the main part's while loop.

Tracking guesses:

1. Add a variable called total_guesses in the do_guess_round function. Add 1 to it each round.

2. Communicate the value stored in this variable to the calling loop by using the return keyword.

Here is the code with changes shown in the comments.

```
"""guess_game_fun
Guess Game with a Function
In this project the guess game is recast using a function"""
import random

PROMPT = 'What is your guess? '

def do_guess_round():
    """Choose a random number, ask the user for a guess
    check whether the guess is true
    and repeat until the user is correct"""
    computers_number = random.randint(1, 100)
    number_of_guesses = 0 # Added
```

```
while True:
    players_guess = raw_input(PROMPT)
    number_of_guesses = number_of_guesses+1  # Added
    if computers_number == int(players_guess):
        print('Correct!')
        return number_of_guesses  # Changed
    elif computers_number > int(players_guess):
        print('Too low')
    else:
        print('Too high')


total_rounds = 0  # Added
total_guesses = 0 # Added

while True:
    total_rounds = total_rounds+1 # Added
    print("Starting round number: "+str(total_rounds)) # Changed
    print("Let the guessing begin!!!")
    this_round = do_guess_round() # Changed
    total_guesses = total_guesses+this_round # Added
    print("You took "+str(this_round)+" guesses") # Added
    avg = str(total_guesses/float(total_rounds)) # Added
    print("Your guessing average = "+avg) # Added
    print("") # blank line
```

Some of the print statements in the while True: loop have been changed and some have been added to give the user some more information about the round. Run the program to see that it works.

The program keeps track of how many guesses have been made while in the function. The main part of the program can't get to the variables within the function. They're local to that function. To get the value back to the main part of the program, they're returned by the return keyword and stored in a variable called this_round.

A running total of guesses is kept by adding this value to the variable called total_guesses. That is then used to calculate the average number of guesses per round (being the total number of guesses divided by the total number of rounds). The `float()` built-in is used to force Python to use decimal (rather than integer) arithmetic. (See Project 3.)

Let the User Quit

The user can quit by typing the letter q. But users don't usually want to quit something by accidentally typing something. So, instead of quitting immediately, a routine asks the user to confirm the quit. The default answer will be yes.

First, the function to confirm the quit:

1. Create a constant (`CONFIRM_QUIT_MESSAGE`) to use as a prompt to confirm the quit.

2. Create a function called `confirm_quit` and write a docstring for it.

3. In the `confirm_quit` function, ask the user to confirm by typing y (using `raw_input`).

   If the user types `"n"`, return the value `False`. Otherwise, return `True`. This looks a little backwards, but works so that the quit is confirmed by default.

This is the code for the `confirm_quit` function:

```
CONFIRM_QUIT_MESSAGE = 'Are you sure you want to quit (Y/n)? '

def confirm_quit():
    """Ask user to confirm that they want to quit
    default to yes
    Return True (yes, quit) or False (no, don't quit) """
    spam = raw_input(CONFIRM_QUIT_MESSAGE)
    if spam == 'n':
        return False
    else:
        return True
```

The player is asked for input and the response is stored in a variable called spam. If spam (what the user typed) is 'n', then the confirm_quit function returns False. That means the program should *abort* (stop) the quit. If spam is anything else (including the user pressing Enter without pressing any other key, or even a capital N), then the function will return True, confirming that the user wants to quit. The function defaults to confirming the quit rather than aborting it. This assumes that most times the user really does want to quit the game.

You could replace the if...else statement with a single line return spam != 'n', but it's complex for now. Stare at it a while until you convince yourself that these are equivalent.

Now you need to integrate that code with the rest of the program:

1. Define a constant QUIT_TEXT to hold the letter q (which is what the user should press if they want to quit).

2. Define a constant QUIT that your do_guess_round function will return if the user is quitting. Assign the value -1 to QUIT.

3. In the do_guess_round function, add a check to see whether the user has typed q rather than a number.

4. If they have, call the confirm_quit function to confirm.

5. If the call to confirm_quit returns a value of True, then quit. Make the code block return QUIT.

   This leaves the function and returns the value of -1. If not, make the code block continue. (That's a new keyword.) Make it the only line in the code block. The continue keyword makes a loop restart at the top of the loop's code block. Depending on the type of loop, this may also mean the loop's counter is incremented.

Add your new constants after import random:

```
QUIT = -1
QUIT_TEXT = 'q'
```

Your new code should go after the `raw_input` line and look something like this:

```
if players_guess == QUIT_TEXT:
    if confirm_quit():
        return QUIT
    else:
        continue # that is, do next round of loop
```

Each time the player guesses, the guess is compared to see if it's the same as `QUIT_TEXT` — that is, q. If it is, then the player is asked to confirm by calling the `confirm_quit` function. If it's confirmed, then `do_guess_round` exits, returning the value of -1 (which is stored in the `QUIT` constant). If it isn't — the user typed q by mistake — `continue` skips the rest of the current iteration of the loop and restarts a new iteration. Since `players_guess` isn't a number (it's q), you'd get an error. For this reason, the rest of the loop needs to be skipped.

The last thing to do is back in `main`. Check whether the value `QUIT` has been returned to the variable `this_round`. If it is returned, do this:

1. Generate a stats message to print.

   Because the code is incrementing `this_round` because it expects the player to guess correctly, it needs to be decremented when the `QUIT` code is returned before you calculate the player's stats. Calculate the player's average number of guesses per round (the total guesses divided by the total number of rounds).

   Make sure you use floating point division or you'll get the wrong answer. Use `float` to convert one of the numbers to floating point.

2. Use `break` to break out of the `while` loop.

3. At the end of the program, print the stats message.

4. Add some `print` statements at the end to print out the statistics.

This code is for Steps 1-4 and goes after the line
`this_round = do_guess_round()`.

```
# new if condition (and code block) to test against quit
if this_round == QUIT:
    total_rounds = total_rounds - 1
    avg = str(total_guesses/float(total_rounds))
    if total_rounds == 0:
        stats_message = 'You completed no rounds. '+\
                        'Please try again later.'
    else:
        stats_message = 'You played ' + str(total_rounds) +\
                        ' rounds, with an average of '+\
                        str(avg)
    break
```

5. Add this code at the bottom of the program (outside the
`while` loop):

```
print(QUIT_MESSAGE)
print(stats_message)
```

Now you get to learn the mysterious reason for assigning -1 to
QUIT. How does `main` tell the difference between a number representing user guesses per round and an instruction to quit?

If the main part of the program isn't sure whether it's getting a
number or a string, it can't use the right test. For example, if you
want to return `quit` as your signal that the user wants to quit,
then `quit` ends up being stored in the `this_round` variable.
Until now, `this_round` has been a number. If you test this number as if it were a string, you get an error that makes Python
crash. You get the same if you test a string as if it were a number.

As you get more familiar with Python, you learn a couple ways to
deal with this. For the moment, though, you can have `do_guess_
round` return a number that can never be a valid number of
guesses. Something like -1 is ideal, since the number of guesses

can never be negative. You could also choose a number like 100,000, on the assumption that no one will ever make that many guesses. My preference is -1.

Overall, in the main part of the program, each time Python returns from the do_guess_round function, it sees if a QUIT value has been returned. If it has, the program prepares some messages to be printed on exit and breaks out of the main while loop. After the messages are printed, the end of the file is reached and the program ends. Phew!

Exiting a Python program

You have exited the program when Python has run out of instructions. The interpreter sort of falls off the end of the program. Sometimes you want the program to exit explicitly. Python has two main ways to force an exit:

✓ A built-in called exit. Use it to exit the Python interpreter's interactive mode. Don't use it in your saved programs because it doesn't clean up properly after itself.

✓ A function called exit. This exit is from the sys module of Python's standard library. To use it, you have to import the sys module like this:

```
# A short program to demonstrate sys.exit
import sys
sys.exit()
print('if you can read this I have not exited when I should
    have')
```

When you run this program from a Python (command line) Shell window, the program should exit without printing out any message. The interpreter never reaches the print statement. This won't work if you run your program from the IDLE Editor window (because of the way IDLE works).

The Complete Code

When you put together all the code, your final program looks like this:

```
"""guess_game_fun
Guess Game with a Fun ction
In this project the guess game is recast using a function"""

import random

PROMPT = 'What is your guess? '

# New constants
QUIT = -1
QUIT_TEXT = 'q'
QUIT_MESSAGE = 'Thank you for playing'
CONFIRM_QUIT_MESSAGE = 'Are you sure you want to quit (Y/n)? '

# New confirm_quit function
def confirm_quit():
    """Ask user to confirm that they want to quit
    default to yes
    Return True (yes, quit) or False (no, don't quit) """
    spam = raw_input(CONFIRM_QUIT_MESSAGE)
    if spam == 'n':
        return False
    else:
        return True


def do_guess_round():
    """Choose a random number, ask the user for a guess
    check whether the guess is true
    and repeat until the user is correct"""
    computers_number = random.randint(1, 100)
    number_of_guesses = 0
```

```python
        while True:
            players_guess = raw_input(PROMPT)
            # new if clause to test against quit
            if players_guess == QUIT_TEXT:
                if confirm_quit():
                    return QUIT
                else:
                    continue # that is, do next round of loop
            number_of_guesses = number_of_guesses+1
            if computers_number == int(players_guess):
                print('Correct!')
                return number_of_guesses
            elif computers_number > int(players_guess):
                print('Too low')
            else:
                print('Too high')


total_rounds = 0
total_guesses = 0

while True:
    total_rounds = total_rounds+1
    print("Starting round number: "+str(total_rounds))
    print("Let the guessing begin!!!")
    this_round = do_guess_round()

    # new if condition (and code block) to test against quit
    if this_round == QUIT:
        total_rounds = total_rounds - 1
        avg = str(total_guesses/float(total_rounds))
        if total_rounds == 0:
            stats_message = 'You completed no rounds. '+\
                            'Please try again later.'
        else:
            stats_message = 'You played ' + str(total_rounds) +\
                            ' rounds, with an average of '+\
                            str(avg)
        break
```

```
total_guesses = total_guesses+this_round
avg = str(total_guesses/float(total_rounds))
print("You took "+str(this_round)+" guesses")
print("Your guessing average = "+str(avg))
print("")


# Added exit messages
print(stats_message)
```

Summary

Wow, you've done a lot. I'm exhausted just reading this list. In this project, you

✔ Met three new keywords: `def`, `return`, `continue`.
(And 9 to go.)

✔ Saw what a function is, and how to create them.

✔ Read the rules about naming functions.

✔ Got to include a docstring in your function, and understand why docstrings are important.

✔ Called a function.

✔ Created function stubs, to keep a record of a function you intend to fill in later.

✔ Saw how variables exist in a parallel dimension when they're in a function and local variables.

✔ Sent information to a function with arguments.

✔ Gave an argument a default value, then saw the difference between positional and keyword arguments.

✔ Got information back from a function with the `return` keyword.

✔ Exited your application.

✔ Created a short function that confirms whether a player really wants to quit your game.

Week 3
Creating Word Games

```
Python 2.7.9 Shell                                          [_][□][X]

File  Edit  Shell  Debug  Options  Windows  Help

Python 2.7.9 (default, Dec 10 2014, 12:24:55) [MSC v.1500 32 bit (Intel)] on win
32
Type "copyright", "credits" or "license()" for more information.
>>> ================================ RESTART ================================
>>>
Tim sneezed the tired hovercraft.
Mrs Pepperpot sneezed the tight dinner.
Some dude threw the slimy hat.
Some dude wrote the tight walk.
Mrs Pepperpot sneezed the Python bag.
My Python teacher stole the big eels.
Dinsdale kissed the furry cat.
Mrs Pepperpot walked the heavy shoes.
Some dude cooked the tall joke.
My Python teacher wrote the silly shirt.
Mrs Pepperpot made the tall book.
Some dude ate the heavy coffee.
My Python teacher climbed the smelly hat.
Dinsdale lost the silly house.
Mrs Pepperpot cooked the funniest laptop.
My Python teacher drank the slippery laptop.
My dad cooked the silly drink.
Dinsdale stole the silly shirt.
A dog wrote the silly car.
A dog walked the heavy eels.
```

This week you're building . . .

Hacker Speaker: 1337 Sp34k3r

Are you ready to write a program turns messages into elite hacker speak (1337 sp34k)? You might've seen where someone replaces letters with numbers or other letters that resemble the original. A common example is using the number 3 to substitute for the letter E.

Idle_debugger.py - C:/Python27/Idle_debugger.py (2.7.9)

File   Edit   Format   Run   Options   Windows   Help

```
""" 1337.py
Given a message, convert it into 1337 sp34k
Brendan Scott
January 2015 """

TEST_MESSAGE = "Hello World!"
##TEST_SUBSTITUTIONS = [['e','3']]
SUBSTITUTIONS = [['a','4'], ['e','3'], ['l','1'], ['o','0'], ['t','7']]

#### Function Section
def encode_message(message, substitutions):
    """Take a string message and apply each of the substitutions provided.
    Substitutions should be a list, the elements of substitutions need to
    be lists of length 2 of the form (old_string, new_string) """
    for s in substitutions:
        old = s[0]
        new = s[1]
        converted = message.replace(old,new)
    return converted

#### Testing Section
message = raw_input("Type the message to be encoded here: ")
converted_text = encode_message(message, SUBSTITUTIONS)
print(message)
print(converted_text)
```

Ln: 18 Col: 30

To do this, you read a heap about strings, lists, objects, and Python introspection. The code in this project is fairly straightforward, but the ideas that it relies on are quite deep. You'll also see how crazy powerful Python is to do such amazing stuff with such simplicity. Everything in this project is something you'll always use in Python!

Waiter, There's An Object In My String

I thought about calling this section "Brain Explosion," because it's so chock-full of information. (My technical editor said she has never witnessed a brain explosion from knowing too much, so I think we're safe.)

You're familiar with strings; you ran into your first string literal back in Project 2. Do you remember that you named your `Hello World` string literal and by naming it you created a variable?

Power up IDLE and do it again right now:

```
>>> my_message = 'Hello World!'
```

Look, my editor's opinions aside (I don't think she has any medical qualifications), you might want to wrap a bandage around your head before proceeding to the next step. Just in case, you know? When you've done that, type this:

```
>>> dir(my_message)
```

Simpson's individual stringettes!

The Monty Python group has a skit where Mr. Simpson has inherited 100,000 miles of string. Unfortunately for him, it's all in little bits. He talks to an advertiser about how to sell it. The skit continues with the advertiser making increasingly ridiculous suggestions (for preventing floods, for example) while Mr. Simpson just can't believe it.

What is going on here? The built-in `dir` is one aspect of Python's Super Introspection Powers! *Introspection* in computing means that the program can tell you stuff about itself. You can tell from the parentheses that `dir` is a function. It takes as an optional argument the name of something and provides you with a directory listing of the thing named as its argument. Clear as mud, right?

The `dir` built-in should've printed out something that looks more or less like this:

```
>>> dir(my_message)
['__add__', '__class__', '__contains__', '__delattr__',
'__doc__', '__eq__', '__format__', '__ge__',
'__getattribute__', '__getitem__', '__getnewargs__',
'__getslice__', '__gt__', '__hash__', '__init__', '__le__',
'__len__', '__lt__', '__mod__', '__mul__', '__ne__',
'__new__', '__reduce__', '__reduce_ex__', '__repr__',
'__rmod__', '__rmul__', '__setattr__', '__sizeof__',
'__str__', '__subclasshook__', '_formatter_field_name_split',
'_formatter_parser', 'capitalize', 'center', 'count',
'decode', 'encode', 'endswith', 'expandtabs', 'find',
'format', 'index', 'isalnum', 'isalpha', 'isdigit', 'islower',
'isspace', 'istitle', 'isupper', 'join', 'ljust', 'lower',
'lstrip', 'partition', 'replace', 'rfind', 'rindex', 'rjust',
'rpartition', 'rsplit', 'rstrip', 'split', 'splitlines',
'startswith', 'strip', 'swapcase', 'title', 'translate',
'upper', 'zfill']
```

These are all names for functions or literals that are associated with your variable `my_message`. When you typed `my_message = 'Hello World!'`, Python got mad busy. It didn't just store `'Hello World!'` somewhere and make `my_message` point to it. No, it did a lot more than that:

✔ It created a *prototype data structure.*

✔ It gave that prototype a name (`my_message`) and assigned `'Hello World!'` to that name.

✔ When it did that, it identified the value as a string. It customized the data structure into one specifically used for string variables.

✔ It looked up a *suite* (group) of standard functions and literals that are useful for strings.

✔ It took that suite and loaded it into the prototype data structure.

Who would've thought that Python would get crazy busy just from that simple line of code? The variable `my_message` is more than just the value `'Hello World!'`. Instead, `my_message` is an *object*. Object is the word that Python uses for the prototype data structure I talked about. It turns out that everything in Python is an object.

TIP

Object types and IDs

I've used the terms *strings* and *lists*. These terms are a shorthand way of saying "objects of type `string`" and "objects of type `list`," respectively. Python has a built-in that tells you the type of an object. Unsurprisingly, it's called `type`:

```
>>> type('a string object')
<type 'str'>
>>> type([])  # that is, an empty list
<type 'list'>
```

All objects have a type. All objects also have an ID. An object's ID is the location where Python is storing the object in memory. You can get an object 's ID by using the `id` built-in:

```
>>> id('a string object')
139900104204840
```

While `type()` always stays the same for any object, its `id` changes often, because Python stores the object in a different place each time you run it.

Every object has a variety of functions and literals. Each of the functions and literals is called an *attribute*. Attributes that are functions are called *methods*. If the function is an attribute of a module, then you just call it a *function* (not a *module method*).

If you were an object (which you aren't), you might have attributes like you.height and you.weight. You might have methods like you.go_clean_your_teeth() or you.go_to_bed(), which your parents could call on you. The height and weight attributes hold *information* about you, while the methods make you *do* something.

Don't forget: Everything in Python is an object.

Dot Your Objects' Attributes

Knowing that my_message has all these attributes, how do you get them? How do you get to, say, the upper method, which is one of the attributes of my_message by dir? The answer is random. (You already did it with random.randint in Project 3. I snuck it in without telling you.) The object in that case was the module called random. You accessed its function randint by joining them together with a dot.

Using this structure, have a look at the help service for the upper method of your variable my_message:

```
>>> help(my_message.upper) # spot the dot?
Help on built-in function upper:

upper(...)
    S.upper() -> string

    Return a copy of the string S converted to uppercase.
```

This is upper's docstring. Can you see why Python docstrings are so awesome? All you do is assign a value to a variable. Then you have an object filled with methods — and you don't need to look in a book or search the Internet to see what they do. The methods themselves tell you what they do.

Try it:

```
>>> my_message.upper
<built-in method upper of str object at 0x7f3d0803e260>
```

That's right, it's a function. To call it, you need to add parentheses: `my_message.upper()`. Think of this as a quick and dirty way to tell whether an attribute is a method.

If you know something is a method, add parentheses to call it.

By the way, notice that the printout confirms it's a method called `upper` of a `str` object, and it's in a specific place in your computer's memory. Call it:

```
>>> my_message.upper()
'HELLO WORLD!'
```

The `upper` function here creates a new, different literal (`'HELLO WORLD!'`) based on the value in `my_message`. The value of `my_message` isn't changed:

```
>>> my_message
'Hello World!'
```

The built-in `dir` lists a lot of attributes for `my_message`. Some of those attributes have names that start with double underscores (like this: `__getslice`). Methods with two underscores are called *private methods;* the others are called *public methods.*

When you're a Python master you can use an object's private methods to do some funky stuff. (You'll do a bit with one of them in the address book project.) For now, ignore private methods. Take a few moments to look at the other attributes of `my_message` and get help on some of its methods.

Reference an attribute of an object by using a dot: `object.attribute`. `object` is the name of the object, and `attribute` is the name of the attribute you want to reference. If the attribute is a method, add parentheses to call the method: `object.attribute` (*<include the method's arguments, if any, here>*).

Dunder

Different people pronounce an attribute name like __init__ different ways. My personal preference is just *dunder init* (for double under init), but if you don't like that, try *underscore underscore init underscore underscore, under under init, double under init,* or *dunder init dunder.*

Meet the List

Did you notice the output of dir(my_message) has those square brackets [] around it? You saw these in the Hello World! project, when you read about range. I told you I'd tell you about the brackets later. It's later.

Square brackets indicate a *list object*. Lists are a form of "container" (like a programming bucket) that can store other objects in a specific order. The objects in the list are called *elements*.

Go Through the Elements of a List

In Project 2 you use the range built-in to create a list and then to *iterate* (go) through each element in the list. It looks like this:

```
>>> range(3)
[0, 1, 2]
>>> for i in range(3):
        print(i)


0
1
2
```

The range(3) is the list [0, 1, 2]. The line for i in range(3): is therefore equal to for i in [0, 1, 2]:. It assigns to i the value of each element in the list one at a time.

There's nothing special about the list being a list of numbers; you can use this `for i in Y` structure for any object (`Y` in this example) that contains other objects. For example, the `dir` built-in gives you a list of strings. (You can tell they're strings because they have single quotes around each of them.)

To print each `my_message` attribute on a separate line, you can do this:

```
>>> for i in dir(my_message):
            print i


    __add__
    __class__
    __contains__
    [...]
```

It doesn't actually print `[...]`. That just shows that I've left stuff out.

Run the program yourself to get the full output. Your Python-is-mad-crazy-alert should be flashing right now as well. If you have any list at all, you can go through each item in the list by entering just a simple line of code — `for element in listname:`.

You can store a list just as you can a literal:

```
>>> string_object_attributes = dir(my_message)
>>> string_object_attributes
['__add__', '__class__', '__contains__', '__delattr__',
'__doc__', '__eq__', '__format__', '__ge__',
'__getattribute__', '__getitem__', '__getnewargs__',
'__getslice__', '__gt__', '__hash__', '__init__', '__le__',
'__len__', '__lt__', '__mod__', '__mul__', '__ne__',
'__new__', '__reduce__', '__reduce_ex__', '__repr__',
'__rmod__', '__rmul__', '__setattr__', '__sizeof__',
'__str__', '__subclasshook__', '_formatter_field_name_split',
'_formatter_parser', 'capitalize', 'center', 'count',
'decode', 'encode', 'endswith', 'expandtabs', 'find',
'format', 'index', 'isalnum', 'isalpha', 'isdigit', 'islower',
```

```
'isspace', 'istitle', 'isupper', 'join', 'ljust', 'lower',
'lstrip', 'partition', 'replace', 'rfind', 'rindex', 'rjust',
'rpartition', 'rsplit', 'rstrip', 'split', 'splitlines',
'startswith', 'strip', 'swapcase', 'title', 'translate',
'upper', 'zfill']
```

Since everything in Python is an object — did I mention that? — you can use the `dir` built-in on this list as well:

```
>>> dir(string_object_attributes)
['__add__', '__class__', '__contains__', '__delattr__',
'__delitem__', '__delslice__', '__doc__', '__eq__',
'__format__', '__ge__', '__getattribute__', '__getitem__',
'__getslice__', '__gt__', '__hash__', '__iadd__', '__imul__',
'__init__', '__iter__', '__le__', '__len__', '__lt__',
'__mul__', '__ne__',' '__new__', '__reduce__', '__reduce_ex__',
'__repr__', '__reversed__', '__rmul__', '__setattr__',
'__setitem__', '__setslice__', '__sizeof__', '__str__',
'__subclasshook__', 'append', 'count', 'extend', 'index',
'insert', 'pop', 'remove', 'reverse', 'sort']
```

I just want you to notice here that these two lists are different. That's because the first list is the attributes of the `my_message` object (which is a string) and the second list is the `string_object_attributes` attributes. The lists are different because the objects are different types. The first is an object of type `string` (technically, the type is `str`) and the second is an object of type `list`. You'll read about the differences of each type as they're introduced. For now just carry the super-heavy knowledge that each object has a type.

Create Your Own List

You can either create a list with elements already in it (like buying a bucket filled with candy), or you can create an empty list (like buying an empty bucket). Sometimes you want an empty bucket and sometimes you want one with candy in it. You can add elements to a list (and remove them) later if you want to. If you want to create a list with elements already in it, do this:

1. Start with an opening square bracket.

2. Put the elements in and separate each one with a comma. Each element can be a literal, a variable, or any other Python object.

3. End with a closing square bracket.

For example, if numbers are candy, this list is premade with candy:

```
>>> new_list = [0, 1, 2]
```

If you don't have elements when you create the list, you can still create a list by skipping Step 2! You get an empty list. Do it like this:

```
>>> new_list2 = []
```

You can add new elements to the end of a list with the append method. All list objects have an append method:

```
>>> new_list2.append('element 0')
>>> new_list2
['element 0']
```

You can mix and match different object types in a list. The list doesn't care what you put in it. The new_list object has numbers in it, but you can add a string to the end of it:

```
>>> new_list = [0, 1, 2]
>>> new_list.append("a string")
>>> new_list
[0, 1, 2, 'a string']
```

append always adds to the end of the list. This example mixes numbers and a string in the same list, but you can put any objects into a list. You can append the list to itself, but don't go there!

A note on terminology

I've seen members of a list called *elements* and *items.* Maybe it doesn't matter, but I use the word *element* to refer to things that make up a list. I use another word, *item,* to refer to things that make up a different data structure (which you meet in the Cryptopy project).

Create a List on Steroids

If you can create the elements in your list from an existing list according to a formula, then Python has a shorthand form for creating it: *list comprehension.* Actually, any iterator will do, but we're talking about lists at the moment.

Create a list comprehension like this:

1. Open with a square bracket.

2. Choose one (or more) dummy variables.

3. Write a formula involving the dummy variables.

4. Follow the formula with a `for` statement for each dummy variable.

5. Close with a square bracket.

For example, if you want the first ten even numbers (starting at 0), you'd use what's in Figure 6-1.

When it runs into this list comprehension, Python

🗸 Creates an empty list.

🗸 Goes through each element in the list generated by `range(10)` and stores its value in a dummy variable named x. That is, it runs through the following numbers in this order — 0, 1, 2, 3, 4, 5, 6, 7, 8, 9. Remember `range` starts from 0.

Formula

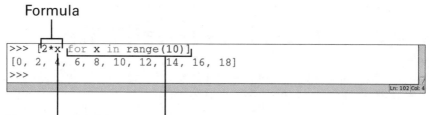

Dummy variable

for <dummy variable> in <iterable>

Figure 6-1: Create the even numbers from 0 to 18 using a list comprehension.

✔ For each, it applies the formula (in this case, 2*x) to the value in x and appends the result to the list.

✔ Finishes creating the list when it has gone through all the elements in range(10).

This is an insanely easy and powerful way to create a new list. List comprehension lets you add conditions as well. This means you can filter out a subset of the elements you're creating. For example, to get all of the even numbers less than 10, you can add a condition at the end of the list comprehension:

```
>>> [x for x in range(10) if x%2 == 0]
[0, 2, 4, 6, 8]
```

Here the condition if x%2 == 0 says that the number is even. On the left side is the modulo operator. It gives the remainder left over after dividing the left side by the right side. (The guessing game project covers this.) If you divide even numbers by 2, the remainder is 0. For each of the even numbers, the if condition will be true and x added. For the odd numbers, it's false and they're skipped.

Test Whether an Element's In a List

You can tell, pretty easily, whether an element is in a list. Just use the in keyword:

```
>>> 0 in [0,1]
True
```

```
>>> 5 in [0,1]
False
```

It's true that the element 0 is in the list [0,1], but false that the number 5 is in that list. You can reverse the logic by using the not keyword:

```
>>> 0 not in [0,1]
False
>>> 5 not in [0,1]
True
```

WARNING!

Watch those return values

Be careful of list methods. They tend to change the list *in place*. This means that, unlike the upper method of my_message, which returns a new string, the list itself might be changed by the method.

This has two main consequences. First, the list itself is changed (duh) and second, the method has no return value. If you try to assign the return value of a method to a variable, the variable ends up being None. But you expected to have a list returned to you. This has caught me more than once. Here's an example using the reverse method of the string type:

```
>>> a_list = range(10)
>>> a_list
[0, 1, 2, 3, 4, 5, 6, 7, 8, 9]
>>> reversed_list = a_list.reverse()
>>> # reverse doesn't return a value!
>>> print(reversed_list)
None
>>> a_list # the list itself has been changed
[9, 8, 7, 6, 5, 4, 3, 2, 1, 0]
```

Normally you'd expect a function to return the value that you want. You expect reversed_list to store the reversed list, but it doesn't — because the method reverse returns a value of None.

Planning Your Elite Hacker Speaker

Your 1337 Sp34k3r needs to do this stuff:

1. Receive a message from the user. (You can use `raw_input` for that.)

2. Run through each letter in that message and, if it's a letter that can be substituted in elite speak, make the substitution.

3. Construct a new message and print it out.

Set Up Your File

Time to start putting together a skeleton of your program. You can fill in the details a little later.

1. Create a file to store your code. Name the file `1337.py`.

   Make sure to include the `.py` ending. Project 4 explains how to create a file if you want a reminder.

2. Write a docstring at the top of the file explaining what the file is supposed to do.

   That's you creating a module docstring.

3. Create a constant called `TEST_MESSAGE` and assign to it a test message string.

4. Create a constant called `TEST_SUBSTITUTIONS`. Assign to it a test substitution to work with. Make this test substitution a list containing one element: `['e','3']`.

   Be careful, this is a trick!

This is what I came up with:

```
""" 1337.py
Given a message, convert it into 1337 sp34k
Brendan Scott
January 2015 """


TEST_MESSAGE = "Hello World!"
TEST_SUBSTITUTIONS = [['e','3']]
```

Did you remember to include double square brackets for the test substitution list? I was serious when I said `['e','3']` is a *single* element. To make a list out of it, you have to put square brackets around it: `[['e','3']]`. Running this program won't do anything interesting, but you change that in a sec.

Create a function stub

The next step is to create a function stub for the function that will code the message into `1337`.

1. Use a block comment (a # hash) to mark a `Functions` section.

2. Think of a name for the function and create a function stub in your new function section.

3. Think of names for two dummy variables that the function will use.

   The function takes a message to code, as well as a list of substitutions to be performed. You're naming those two variables.

4. Add a docstring to explain what the function is doing.

5. Use a block comment to mark a `Testing` section in your code.

6. In the `Testing` section, add a call to the function using the test variables you created. Assign the return value from this call to a variable.

7. Print the variable.

I came up with this:

```
#### Functions Section
def encode_message(message, substitutions):
    """Take a string message and apply each of the substitutions
    provided. Substitutions should be a list, the elements of
    substitutions need to be lists of length 2 of the form
    (old_string, new_string) """

#### Testing Section
converted_text = encode_message(TEST_MESSAGE, TEST_SUBSTITUTIONS)
print(converted_text)
```

Run the code

Save the file and run the code: Press F5 or choose Run ⇨ Run Module from the menu. Are there any problems so far? You should get this output in the interactive Shell:

```
>>> ================================= RESTART
=================================
>>>
None
```

Not much, is it? Because the function `encode_message` doesn't use the `return` keyword, the value assigned to the variable `converted_text` is None. Makes sense. You've established the basic program flow to *and* from the `encode_message` function.

You could have had the function return the message it was passed (probably not good because it wouldn't flag that it was ignoring any substitutions) or returned a debugging message like `"Function not implemented yet!"` or returned None. I prefer not returning a value at the stub stage. I just find it easier, but it depends a little on the situation.

Make Code Letter Substitutions

The next task is to take `encode_message` and make it *do*
something: replace letters. To change a string like `speak` to
`sp34k`, replace the specific letters in the string. It just so
happens that strings (objects of the `str` type) have their own
method called `replace`. Find out what it does by looking at its
docstring:

```
>>> my_message = 'Hello World!'
>>> help(my_message.replace)
Help on built-in function replace:

replace(...)
    S.replace(old, new[, count]) -> string

    Return a copy of string S with all occurrences of substring
    old replaced by new.  If the optional argument count is
    given, only the first count occurrences are replaced.
```

Use your existing `my_message` text as a test message. According
to the documentation that you have just printed out in the code
readout only two lines previous, in order to use this method you
need to have two string variables, one named `old`, the other
named `new`. These are fed into the method as arguments.

```
>>> my_message = 'Hello World!'
>>> old = 'e'
>>> new = '3' # remember the quotes
>>> new_string = my_message.replace(old,new)
>>> new_string
'H3llo World!'
```

A new copy of the string `Hello World!` was created. Then (actually, while it was being created), the `e` in `Hello` was replaced by a
3 (and stored in `new_string`). The original variable `my_message`
remains unchanged. It's important that both `old` and `new` are

strings; however, you don't need to save them into separate variables. Using bare string literals will still work:

```
>>> new_string = my_message.replace('e','3')
>>> new_string
'H3llo World!'
```

Don't feel like you're forced to needlessly create variables to fill names in a method's documentation. That said, I've chosen to use `old` and `new` because it will make the logic a little easier later.

Replace a Letter

Now fill in the replacement code in the function itself. The function needs to

1. Iterate (go through) each substitution it's given.

   I say *each* because the function is written to receive a list of substitutions. I know that you're only testing it with one substitution. When you're coding, you need to anticipate the general case.

   ```
   for s in substitutions:
   ```

2. Unpack each substitution.

   You get it as a list of two strings. You need to unpack the list to separate strings to give them to the `replace` method.

   ```
   old = s[0]
   new = s[1]
   ```

3. Use the `replace()` method of the message variable to apply each of the substitutions.

   ```
   converted = message.replace(old,new)
   ```

4. Return the encoded message.

   ```
   return converted
   ```

Here's the code so far:

```
""" 1337.py
Given a message, convert it into 1337 sp34k
Brendan Scott
January 2015 """


TEST_MESSAGE = "Hello World!"
TEST_SUBSTITUTIONS = [['e','3']]


#### Function Section
def encode_message(message, substitutions):
    """Take a string message and apply each of the substitutions
    provided. Substitutions should be a list, the elements of
    substitutions need to be lists of length 2 of the form
    (old_string, new_string) """
    for s in substitutions:
        old = s[0]
        new = s[1]
        converted = message.replace(old,new)

    return converted

#### Testing Section
converted_text = encode_message(TEST_MESSAGE, TEST_SUBSTITUTIONS)
print(TEST_MESSAGE)
print(converted_text)
```

When it runs, you get this:

```
>>> ================================= RESTART
==============================
>>>
Hello World!
H3llo World!
```

Everything seems to work fine. However, this code has a logical error. It works with the test substitution you set up, but fails when you try to generalize it. Have a think about what the problem is and how you would solve it. All will be revealed in a moment!

Errors in program logic are hard to spot. The Python interpreter can't see them because the code is valid — it just doesn't do what you want it to do. They come up mainly because you misunderstand how Python is flowing through your program, or because you misunderstand what values your variables are taking.

You're super familiar with the code you've written and people tend to make assumptions about what their code's actually doing. Explaining your problem in words (talking to your goldfish/pet rock/balloon with a face drawn on it/blank wall/unsuspecting relative) helps break you out of this way of thinking. If you can, go through this book with a coding buddy. You can talk to each other about the issues you find.

Let the User Enter a Message

You know how to get text input from a user. You did it in Project 3:

1. Get a text message from the user using `raw_input`.

2. Assign the user's input to a variable.

3. Pass that variable to the `encode_message` function.

4. Print out the message to be encoded.

5. Print the output of the call to `encode_message`.

```
""" 1337.py
Given a message, convert it into 1337 sp34k
Brendan Scott
January 2015 """

TEST_MESSAGE = "Hello World!"
TEST_SUBSTITUTIONS = [['e','3']]
```

```
#### Function Section
def encode_message(message, substitutions):
    for s in substitutions:
    """Take a string message and apply each of the substitutions
    provided. Substitutions should be a list, the elements of
    substitutions need to be lists of length 2 of the form
    (old_string, new_string) """
        old = s[0]
        new = s[1]
        converted = message.replace(old,new)
    return converted


#### Testing Section
message = raw_input("Type the message to be encoded here: ")
converted_text = encode_message(message, TEST_SUBSTITUTIONS)
print(message)
print(converted_text)
```

Did you remember to change the final print from TEST_MESSAGE to message?

Run the program to make sure it works. Type your own message if you like, but make sure it has at least one *e* in it, or nothing will happen.

```
>>> ================================= RESTART
=================================
>>>
Type the message to be encoded here: Python is awesome
Python is awesome
Python is aw3som3
```

Define Letter Substitutions

Changing all the *e*s to *3*s won't cut the mustard with your h4ck3r friends. You need more! More, I tell you! The elite speak substitutions that I suggest are set out here. But this is your project, so freestyle it if you want to.

Letter	Substitute By
a	4
e	3
l	1
o	0
t	7

You can code each of these substitutions as a list, with the order in the list having a meaning. For example: `['a','4']` stores the letter to be replaced as the first item (at location 0) and the letter to replace with the second item (at location 1). You can't write `[a,4]` because Python will think a is the name of a variable rather than a string.

You could write these substitutions like this:

```
['a','4'], ['e','3'], ['l','1'], ['o','0'], ['t','7']
```

Create your substitutions list by putting square brackets around all of this. Here is how you do it with some code that prints out each of the elements:

```
>>> substitutions = [['a','4'], ['e','3'], ['l','1'], ['o','0'],
                     ['t','7']]
>>> for s in substitutions:
        print s
```

```
['a', '4']
['e', '3']
['l', '1']
['o', '0']
['t', '7']
```

I used the trick I mentioned to print out each of the elements in the list named substitutions. Just to recap:

⯈ This list has five elements.

⯈ Each of these elements is itself a list. Each of these lists only has two elements.

⯈ Each of those two elements is a string, and each of those strings has only one character in it.

Why have I asked you to create a list called substitutions when there's only *one* substitution? At the moment we're keeping it simple. The code will be written so that it doesn't matter how many elements there are. For example, in the for loop for s in substitutions:, the code works the same whether there is one substitution in the list or five.

You write the code with a single substitution for testing. When things work for one substitution, you change the code to deal with multiple substitutions by adding more.

It's awesome to be filled with inspiration and pound out line after line of code. But unless you're perfect — and no one is — those lines of code will have errors. The more lines you produce without testing, the harder it is to find the errors. Break your code into parts and prove each part separately. Join two parts together, then test that join.

Apply all the Substitutions

When everything is in order and the code seems to work for a single substitution, you can use all the substitutions set out earlier:

1. Add a constant SUBSTITUTIONS and assign to it the substitutions given earlier.

2. Pass SUBSTITUTIONS to the encoding function.

3. Delete the test variables.

Or, you can keep them for future testing.

```
""" 1337.py
Given a message, convert it into 1337 sp34k
Brendan Scott
January 2015 """


TEST_MESSAGE = "Hello World!"
##TEST_SUBSTITUTIONS = [['e','3']]
SUBSTITUTIONS = [['a', '4'], ['e', '3'], ['l', '1'], ['o', '0'],
                 ['t', '7']]


#### Function Section
def encode_message(message, substitutions):
    """Take a string message and apply each of the substitutions
    provided. Substitutions should be a list, the elements of
    substitutions need to be lists of length 2 of the form
    (old_string, new_string) """
    for s in substitutions:
        old = s[0]
        new = s[1]
        converted = message.replace(old,new)
    return converted


#### Testing Section
message = raw_input("Type the message to be encoded here: ")
converted_text = encode_message(message, SUBSTITUTIONS)
print(message)
print(converted_text)
```

This sample code is what you use later with the IDLE debugger. Now that that's done, you can triumphantly run your 1337 speaker:

```
>>> ================================= RESTART
================================
>>>
Type the message to be encoded here: Python is awesome
Python is awesome
Py7hon is awesome
```

Oh. That isn't supposed to happen. The os are supposed to be 0s and the es are supposed to be 3s, and so on. One substitution worked — t->7. The logic error has come back to bite me. How come just one substitution is being applied?

Use `print` to Debug the Code

Thanks to a woman named Grace Hopper, the process of removing errors from code is known as *debugging*. Debugging is a skill. The more you do it, the better you'll get.

Try these strategies to debug this code:

✔ Include a `print` statement to output relevant data. What's relevant will change depending on what's going on. Start with the data that the program is manipulating when the error occurs and move out from there.

✔ Add `print` statements into the code to track what's going on where. For example, add `print("I've just entered function X")` or `print("Leaving function X")` at the start and end of function X. These help you understand the program's flow.

✔ Vary the SUBSTITUTIONS constant to see what effect that has on the replacements.

✔ Be watchful. *The place where the error is revealed isn't always where the error is.* Backtrack through how the program got to the point where the error showed itself and look for errors there.

That's the strategy you use here. Now:

1. Include one or more `print` statements somewhere in the program.

2. Make each `print` statement print either a variable or the location within the program that has been reached — like `print("Leaving encode_message")`.

3. Run the program and review the output to see what's going on.

Python logging

A logging module is available for large programs. This module writes (logs) all your messages into a file that you can inspect later. The file has details too, such as the time the message was logged and the line number in the program where the logging occurred. These details are very useful, but aren't there when you use a `print` statement.

I came up with this. Look at the comments to see what's been changed:

```python
""" 1337.py
Given a message, convert it into 1337 sp34k
Brendan Scott
January 2015 """


TEST_MESSAGE = "Hello World!"
##TEST_SUBSTITUTIONS = [['e','3']]
SUBSTITUTIONS = [['a', '4'], ['e', '3'], ['l', '1'], ['o', '0'],
                 ['t', '7']]


#### Function Section
def encode_message(message, substitutions):
    """Take a string message and apply each of the substitutions
    provided. Substitutions should be a list, the elements of
    substitutions need to be lists of length 2 of the form
    (old_string, new_string) """
    for s in substitutions:
        old = s[0]
        new = s[1]
        converted = message.replace(old,new)
        print("converted text = "+converted) # Added
    print("Leaving encode_message")  # Added

    return converted
```

```
#### Testing Section
message = raw_input("Type the message to be encoded here: ")
converted_text = encode_message(message, SUBSTITUTIONS)
print("started with "+message) # Changed
print("Converted to "+converted_text) # Changed
```

In this code I added two `print` statements. The first shows the value of the string converted after each replacement. (Check out the indentation levels of the various `print` statements.) As you know, the indentation level determines whether the statement is inside or outside the code block. The second, which reads `print("Leaving encode_message")`, shows where the program leaves the `encode_message` function.

When you run this code, you get this output:

```
>>> ================================ RESTART
================================
>>>
Type the message to be encoded here: Python is awesome
converted text = Python is 4wesome
converted text = Python is aw3som3
converted text = Python is awesome
converted text = Pyth0n is awes0me
converted text = Py7hon is awesome
Leaving encode_message
started with Python is awesome
Converted to Py7hon is awesome
```

I guessed earlier that only the last replacement worked because that showed up in the earlier `print` statements (last two lines in this readout). I was wrong! This printout shows that each replacement is happening correctly — but they keep being made to the original string, so they're not *cumulative*. Each substitution is new, rather than being made to the output of the previous substitution.

This is an example of a problem with the programming logic. Rather than working on the string-as-substituted, each substitution operated on the original string, pretty much getting rid of the earlier work.

You can solve this by getting rid of the variable converted in the function encode_message. Instead, you store the replaced text back into the message variable. However, you have to remember to change the print functions that refer to converted to message. You also need to return message, rather than converted. Make these changes and run your code. Yup, you *can* work those changes out for yourself. Don't run screaming from the room.

You should get this code:

```
""" 1337.py
Given a message, convert it into 1337 sp34k
Brendan Scott
January 2015 """

TEST_MESSAGE = "Hello World!"
##TEST_SUBSTITUTIONS = [['e','3']]
SUBSTITUTIONS = [['a','4'], ['e','3'], ['l','1'], ['o','0'],
                 ['t','7']]


#### Function Section
def encode_message(message, substitutions):
    """Take a string message and apply each of the substitutions
            provided.
    Substitutions should be a list, the elements of substitutions
            need to
    be lists of length 2 of the form (old_string, new_string) """
    for s in substitutions:
        old = s[0]
        new = s[1]
        message = message.replace(old,new) # Changed
        print("converted text = "+message)
    print("Leaving encode_message") # Changed
```

```
    return message # Changed

#### Testing Section
message = raw_input("Type the message to be encoded here: ")
converted_text = encode_message(message, SUBSTITUTIONS)
print("started with "+message)
print("Converted to "+converted_text)
```

This code should give you this output:

```
>>> ================================= RESTART
================================
>>>
Type the message to be encoded here: Python is awesome
converted text = Python is 4wesome
converted text = Python is 4w3som3
converted text = Python is 4w3som3
converted text = Pyth0n is 4w3s0m3
converted text = Py7h0n is 4w3s0m3
Leaving encode_message
started with Python is awesome
Converted to Py7h0n is 4w3s0m3
```

Go back and remove the `print` statements that you put in for debugging. You can do this either by literally deleting them or by putting a hash (#) in front of them.

Remember, hashes (#) comment out the code that follows on that line.

Debug with IDLE's Debugger

IDLE has an *integrated* debugger. It can stop the code at fixed points (called *breakpoints*) and step through what's there. The debugger also shows you the values of the variables. A detailed review of the debugger is beyond the scope of this book, but here's a quick taste. If you like it investigate further!

Mac users: IDLE's debugger might work properly or it might not. It depends on what Mac you have and what version of Python was loaded on it and, possibly, the phase of the moon. Try Cmd-click instead of right-click. If that doesn't work, you'll have to skip this bit.

1. Go back to the code at the end of the steps in "Apply All the Substitutions."

2. Open a new file in IDLE and copy this code into it.

3. Save the file as `idle_debugger.py`.

4. On the IDLE Shell window, choose Debug ⇨ Debugger.

   This brings up the Debug Control window shown in Figure 6-2.

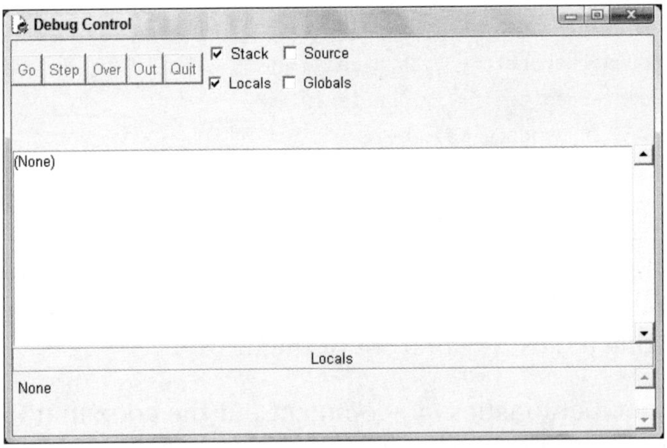

Figure 6-2: IDLE's Debug Control window looks like this.

5. Go to the IDLE Editor window. Right-click line 18 and select Set Breakpoint.

   Mac users: Try Cmd-click, knowing that it might not work.

   You can see the line number in the bottom-right corner in Figure 6-3. When you set the breakpoint, the line of code where you set it is highlighted in yellow.

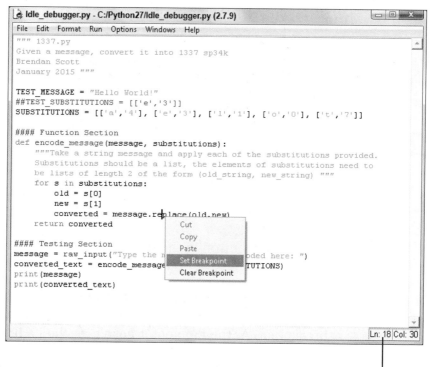

Current line number

Figure 6-3: Set a breakpoint from the menu.

6. With the breakpoint set, run the code as your normally would.

Instead of running the whole code, IDLE prepares to start at the start of the file and then gives control to the Debug Control window. The window used to be drab and boring, but now it springs to life! In a boring sort of way. See Figure 6-4.

The Debug Control window tells you:

- That you're on line 4 of `idle_debugger.py`.

- That the code you're about to run ends with: `January 2015"""`. (If the line is short enough, you'll see all the code on the line.)

- The values of local variables (in the Locals part of the window).

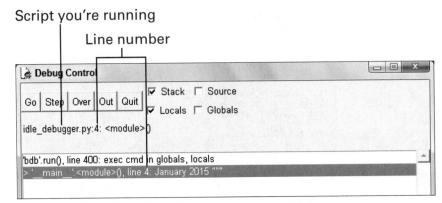

Script you're running

Line number

Figure 6-4: The Debug Control window springs to life!

7. Click the Go button in the top-left corner of the Debug Control window.

The `raw_input` line had asked you for input in the IDLE Shell window. Go tells Python to run the code until it reaches a breakpoint. At the moment it hasn't reached a breakpoint, but it has hit a `raw_input` line, and the program needs some text before it can continue.

8. Go to that window and type `"Python is awesome"` in the prompt. Then press Enter. See Figure 6-5 for what happens.

The Debug Control window has changed a bit now. It now tells you:

- That you're on line 18, in a function called `encode_message()`.

- The values of all the variables being used within `encode_message()` in the Locals part of the window. This substitution is `['a', '4']`, that the value of `new` is `'4'`, and that the value of `old` is `'a'`.

9. Click the Go button again.

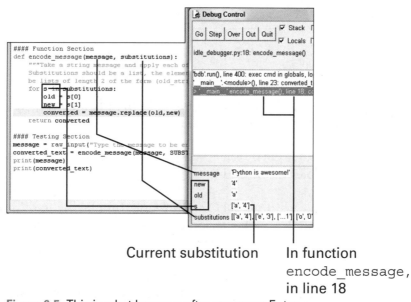

Current substitution   In function
`encode_message`,
in line 18

Figure 6-5: This is what happens after you press Enter.

The code runs until it reaches a breakpoint. Because the breakpoint is in a loop, the code stops on the next iteration of the loop. You can see in the Locals section that a new local, called `converted`, has been added to the list of locals. You can also see that the value of `message` hasn't changed.

Pressing the Go button again makes the same thing happen again. The local message doesn't change. And even though `converted` changed (the *es* have been replaced), in the previous pass the *a* was a *4;* now it's been changed back. By now you'd probably have *twigged* (which means worked out, where I come from) that you're not updating the message variable (which you noticed when you used `print` to print out the values).

Play around with the other buttons to see what they do.

 Get rid of breakpoints by right-clicking (Mac users: Try Cmd-click) the line where the breakpoint is and clicking Clear Breakpoint. To turn off the debugger, choose Debug ➪ Debugger from the IDLE Shell window.

Summary

In this project you read a lot about objects, lists, and debugging techniques. You

- Discovered that everything in Python is an object and that there are different types.

- Read that each object has a unique ID, which records where the object is stored in the computer's memory.

- Worked with objects that have attributes. Some of those attributes are like variables or literals, and others are like functions. (These attributes are called *methods.*)

- Referred to an attribute called `attribute_name` of an object called `object_name` by using the dot syntax: `object_name.attribute_name`. Add parentheses and arguments if it's a method (called `method_name`): `object_name.method_name(argument_name)`.

- Saw some methods of list objects change the list *in place.* Watch those: They give you a return value of `None`.

- Created a new data type — the list — and learned that lists have elements.

- Created a list with a list comprehension and using a conditional.

- Used `in` to test whether a certain value is an element of a list. To test that it *isn't* an element, you used `not in`. (Both are keywords!)

- Used the `replace` method of string objects.

- Debugged code using `print` statements and by using the IDLE debugger.

- Set breakpoints to stop code using the IDLE debugger.

- Inspected the values of local variables as code is running.

Cryptopy

The muscles you used in the 1337 sp34k3r project get flexed in this project, too. You encrypt and decrypt messages using Python and a little something called a Caesar Cipher.

D	E	F	...	X	Y	Z	A	B	C
A	B	C	...	U	V	W	X	Y	Z

Julius Caesar was a Roman general. *Ciphers* are what real-life spies use to make and break codes. A cipher is a procedure or a device that changes readable text (called *plaintext*) into unreadable text (called *ciphertext*). Caesar *encrypted,* or coded, his messages by shifting letters along the alphabet. If he had a plaintext *d,* he would replace it with an *a.* For an *e* he would write *b,* and so on.

Printable characters

How do you get the printable characters? The `string` module from the standard library includes a list of all of the printable characters as one of its attributes. Type the following to see them:

```
>>> import string
>>> string.printable
'0123456789abcdefghijklmnopqrstuvwxyzABCDEFGHIJKLMNOPQRSTUVWXYZ
!"#$%&\'()*+,-./:;<=>?@[\\]^_`{|}~ \t\n\r\x0b\x0c'
```

Everything seems sensible except for the last few. What are all the slashes? These are characters you need to know:

`\\`	slash \
`\t`	tab
`\n`	new line
`\r`	carriage return

The slash is an *escape code.* When Python sees a slash, it looks at the next character and prints something based on that. When it prints a string with \n in it, it doesn't print \ or n. Instead, it prints a new line. Type the following to see them in practice:

```
>>> print("1\t2")
1       2
>>> print("1\n2")
1
2
```

In this project you

✔ Take a plaintext message.

✔ Encrypt the message.

✔ Present the encrypted message.

✔ Decrypt a ciphertext message into plaintext.

✔ Present the plaintext.

Your cipher is going to handle uppercase and lowercase letters, plus punctuation marks and numbers. Caesar got off easy. He didn't have to worry about punctuation or uppercase letters.

Slice Off Those Dud Characters

None of the characters from \t onwards are needed for the encryption regime. For example, if you're encrypting a new line you probably want to keep it as a new line, rather than change it to a letter. Conversely, if your ciphertext contains a new line you probably don't think that's significant to the meaning of the plaintext. Everything else in `string.printable` is fine except for that slice of slashes at the end.

How do you create a string that has everything except that slice? Python has an operator `[:]` (square brackets and a colon) that slices up strings or lists.

Here is an example:

```
>>> test_string = '0123456789'
>>> test_string[0:1]
'0'
>>> test_string[1:3]
'12'
>>> # range(10) is a list of the numbers from 0 to 9 inclusive
>>> range(10)[0:1]
```

```
[0]
>>> range(10)[1:3]
[1, 2]
>>> test_string[:3]
'012'
>>> test_string[3:]
'3456789'
```

The slicing operator takes the form *string_name*[a:b]. (Instead of *string_name,* type the actual name of the variable to slice.) a is the *index* (the number that shows how far into the string) of the start of the slice, and b is the index of the end of the slice. In the string '0123456789', each character is also its index. The string '0' is at index 0, the string '3' is at index 3, and so on. In the string 'Hello', the letter 'H' is at index 0, 'e' is at index 1, and so on.

You get the characters starting at character number a up to, but not including, character number b. This might be a little confusing since the characters start at 0. What's more, the numbers a and b can be negative. If they are, then they are counted from the end of the string.

```
>>> # everything up to, but not including, the last character
>>> test_string[:-1]
'012345678'
>>> test_string[-1:] # everything *from* the last character
'9'
```

It's actually pretty easy to get the printable characters less those strange ones at the end. Just slice them off by taking all the characters up to the fifth from the end. This code slices off the last five characters and saves the rest into a variable char_set holding the set of characters to be encoded:

```
>>> char_set = string.printable[:-5]
>>> char_set
'0123456789abcdefghijklmnopqrstuvwxyzABCDEFGHIJKLMNOPQRSTUVWXYZ
!"#$%&\'()*+,-./:;<=>?@[\\]^_`{|}~ '
```

This is the list of characters that you're going to encode.

TIP

You can slice a list in the same way as you slice a string, except that, with a list, the things you're slicing are elements, not characters.

Make a Substitution Table

Did you ever send a coded message to your friend? Have you sent a text that your parents thought sounded like code? (tbh, they don't use brb or ttyl, do they?)

Assign a character to each character in the plaintext message. Caesar's cipher substituted (say that six times quickly) the letter *a* for the letter *d*. That means shifting the alphabet three characters to the left. How can you do that?

Figure 7-1 shows how the characters are changed. Caesar would go through each letter in his message, find it in the top row, then write the letter below it on the paper he gave to his messenger. If his first plaintext word was BAD, then the ciphertext would be YXA.

D	E	F	...	X	Y	Z	A	B	C
A	B	C	...	U	V	W	X	Y	Z

Figure 7-1: That's one sick cipher, Caesar.

In this example you're working with a shift of three, so slice off three characters from the front of `char_set` and add them to the end. If you want to encrypt with a different shift, choose a different number.

This code creates your substitution characters from the base character set, then prints them out so you can have a look at them:

```
>>> substitution_chars = char_set[-3:]+char_set[:-3]
>>> substitution_chars
'}~ 0123456789abcdefghijklmnopqrstuvwxyzABCDEFGHIJKLMNOPQRSTUVWXYZ
!"#$%&\'()*+,-./:;<=>?@[\\]^_`{|'
```

Then you have your code. (Get it?) The first line shows the letter as it appears in the plaintext of a message. The next line has the ciphertext characters you'll use to write your message. (Just the first 62 are here.)

```
>>> print(char_set[:62]+'\n'+substitution_chars[:62])
0123456789abcdefghijklmnopqrstuvwxyzABCDEFGHIJKLMNOPQRSTUVWXYZ
}~ 0123456789abcdefghijklmnopqrstuvwxyzABCDEFGHIJKLMNOPQRSTUVW
```

To see the full list, open the IDLE Shell window and type `print(char_set+'\n'+substitution_chars)`.

Set Up Your Cipher

Time now to do the basic stuff:

1. Create a file called `cryptopy.py`.

2. Write a module docstring at the top of the file.

3. Create an `Imports` section and import the `string` module.

   ```
   #### Imports Section
   import string
   ```

4. Create a `Constants` section and use the code to create `char_set` and `substitution_chars`. But change their names so that they are `ALLCAPS` (since they're supposed to be constants).

   ```
   #### Constants Section
   CHAR_SET = string.printable[:-5]
   SUBSTITUTION_CHARS = CHAR_SET[-3:]+CHAR_SET[:-3]
   ```

5. Create a constant called `TEST_MESSAGE` and store a test message in it. You'll use it for testing.

   ```
   TEST_MESSAGE = "I like Monty Python.  They are very funny."
   ```

6. Create a `Functions` section and in it, create a function stub called `encrypt_msg` that takes one argument (the plaintext to be encrypted). Include a docstring.

   Project 5 explains how to make a function stub. You can go back there if you need a reminder.

   ```
   #### Function Section
   def encrypt_msg(plaintext):
       """Take a plaintext message and encrypt each character using
       a Caesar cipher (d->a). Return the cipher text"""

       return plaintext # no encrypting atm
   ```

7. Create a `Testing` section and call the function stub passing the constant `TEST_MESSAGE` to it.

   ```
   #### Testing Section
   ciphertext = encrypt_msg(TEST_MESSAGE)
   ```

You should get something like this:

```
"""Cryptopy
Take a plaintext message and encrypt it using a Caesar cipher
Brendan Scott, 2015
"""


#### Imports Section
import string


#### Constants Section
CHAR_SET = string.printable[:-5]
SUBSTITUTION_CHARS = CHAR_SET[-3:]+CHAR_SET[:-3]


TEST_MESSAGE = "I like Monty Python.  They are very funny."


#### Function Section
def encrypt_msg(plaintext):
    """Take a plaintext message and encrypt each character using
    a Caesar cipher (d->a). Return the cipher text"""
```

```
                    return plaintext # no encrypting atm


     #### Testing Section
     ciphertext = encrypt_msg(TEST_MESSAGE)
     print(TEST_MESSAGE) # for comparison while testing
     print(ciphertext)
```

Run your program just to see if there are any mistakes. If you do make mistakes, make sure your code looks the same as the code here. Also try the debugging methods you used in Project 6.

Use the Dictionary

You use the `replace` method in the l33t sp34k3r project. You're not going to use `replace` in this case because

- Here it's an ugly *ad hoc* (short-term) solution. The l33t sp34k3r project has a handful of characters to change. Here, you have to swap every character. Aim for beautiful code. You read that right — beautiful.

- The solution is harder to generalize. For example, if you want to use a different encryption shift, such as c→a, then you have to rewrite both the encryption function and the decryption function. Forget that!

Use a data type that, if you feed in a d will give you back an a. Python has that kind of data type — a *dictionary*. In this case the d is called the *key* and the a is called the *value*.

You create a dictionary by using curly braces { }. Here's an example, using a key `'d'` and a value `'a'`. In this example, the dictionary is on the right side (`{'d':'a'}`) and the name of a variable (`my_dictionary`) is on the left. You can use any valid variable name here.

```
>>> my_dictionary={'d':'a'}
>>> my_dictionary['d']
'a'
```

Look up a value in a dictionary by putting its corresponding key in square brackets. In this code, the key is `'d'`. To get the value `'a'` from this dictionary, type `my_dictionary['d']`. If you pass a value to the dictionary, it will complain (unless by luck there's a key with the same name). In this example, `my_dictionary` has one item: (`'d':'a'`). That item has a key `'d'` and the value `'a'`. I asked for `my_dictionary['d']` and got the value a.

I'm using the word *element* for the thing that lists have and the word *item* for the thing that dictionaries have. Elements have only one part (their value), but items always have two parts: a key and a value.

Dictionaries in Python have their own methods. (Did I tell you everything in Python is an object?) They're `items`, `keys`, and `values` which, when called, give you the information about the dictionary. For example, to get the items in `my_dictionary`, type `my_dictionary.items()`. Try each of these methods now on `my_dictionary` and make sure you understand the output you're getting.

You can create a dictionary with a number of items in the curly braces, but make sure you separate each item by a comma. Each item needs to be in this form — `<key>:<value>`.

A value can be just about anything. For keys, use either a string or a number. (You can use other things, but stick to strings and numbers for now.)

The comments in the following code tell you what's going on:

```
>>> # an empty dictionary
>>> my_empty_dictionary = {}
>>> # earlier example, dictionary with one item
>>> my_dictionary={'d':'a'}
>>> # dictionary with two items separated by a comma
>>> my_dictionary={'d':'a', 'e':'b'}
```

Python complains if you try to get a key that doesn't exist:

```
>>> my_dictionary['f']

Traceback (most recent call last):
  File "<pyshell#45>", line 1, in <module>
    my_dictionary['f']
KeyError: 'f'
```

After you create a dictionary, you can add to or change the items by assigning a value to the relevant key — either an existing key (changing the value associated with it) or a new key (creating a new item). When you use dictionaries, you don't often have to assign values using bare strings. Instead, you're usually getting the data from another source, storing it in dummy variables, and then using those dummy variables for the assignment. It's conventional to refer to the key by a dummy variable called k and to the corresponding value by a dummy variable called v.

Here's an example:

```
>>> k = 'f'
>>> v = 'c'
>>> my_dictionary[k]=v # create a new item in the existing dictionary
>>> my_dictionary
{'e': 'b', 'd': 'a', 'f': 'c'}
```

Create an Encryption Dictionary

Time to harness the dictionary's power (it's over nine thousaa-aand!). You're going to create a dictionary where every character in CHAR_SET is a key and the matching value is what that character should be changed to.

To do this, you need to know about the enumerate built-in. If you have a list, enumerate will create a new numbered object from it.

Because you can treat a string as a list, this is what happens when you use enumerate("Hello"):

```
>>> [x for x in enumerate("Hello")]
[(0, 'H'), (1, 'e'), (2, 'l'), (3, 'l'), (4, 'o')]
```

This code has created a list of pairs that give the index of each letter in the string "Hello". You can use this in a for loop to run through the elements of a list and get their index at the same time.

```
>>> for i,c in enumerate("Hello"):
        print(i,c)
```

```
(0, 'H')
(1, 'e')
(2, 'l')
(3, 'l')
(4, 'o')
```

In this code, each element created by enumerate is unpacked into two separate dummy variables (i and c). The i is the index of the character stored in c.

Use enumerate in this project to link the plaintext character set to the encrypted characters in the substitution list. They've been created this way:

1. Name your dictionary.

2. Create an empty dictionary with that name.

   Now you're going to assign values to keys.

3. Use for i,k in enumerate(CHAR_SET) to iterate through each character in it.

4. Set each character to a dummy variable k (for key).

   Earlier, you used c (for character) in this project. Use k from now on.

5. Use the index i to get the corresponding character from SUBSTITUTION_CHARS and assign it to a dummy variable v (for value).

6. Create an item by assigning the value v to the key k.

How did it go? I added this in the Constants section at the top of the file after the entry that creates SUBSTITUTION_CHARS:

```
# generate encryption dictionary from the character set and
# its substitutions
encrypt_dict = {}
for i,k in enumerate(CHAR_SET):
    v = SUBSTITUTION_CHARS[i]
    encrypt_dict[k]=v
```

Use a join

To encrypt an entire message, you have to change every character in the message. Unfortunately, strings are *immutable;* you can't change them. You'll build a new string, one character at a time.

A simple way to create the string is by adding new bits one at a time, like this:

```
>>> a_string = ""
>>> a_string
''
>>> for i in range(10):
        a_string = a_string + str(i) # add '0' then '1' and so on


>>> a_string
'0123456789'
```

WARNING!

Joining strings together like this is called *concatenation*. The main thing to know about concatenation is — don't do it. If your life depends on it, or you need a quick fix for a `print` statement, fine. Otherwise don't. Just. Don't. What's happening is that for each iteration of the `for` loop, Python creates a new string, copies across the old string, and adds a single character to it. It's adding ten characters but in the process it makes ten copies. This copying takes too long.

The proper Pythonic way of making a new string from a number of individual characters (or even other strings) is to add all the characters to a list and then join them all together to make a string.

Here's the same example using the `join` method. It's a method of any string. First you store all the characters in a dummy list called `accumulator`, then you join them up using the `join` method of the empty string:

```
>>> accumulator = []
>>> for i in range(10):
        accumulator.append(str(i))


>>> accumulator
['0', '1', '2', '3', '4', '5', '6', '7', '8', '9']
>>> ''.join(accumulator)
'0123456789'
```

You can use any string you like to join the elements of a list. In this example you use the empty string, but you can use another string and it will be included between each element of the list when it's joined.

Here you use the string `' spam, '` to join the accumulator from the previous example:

```
>>> ' spam, '.join(accumulator)
'0 spam, 1 spam, 2 spam, 3 spam, 4 spam, 5 spam, 6 spam, 7 spam,
8 spam, 9'
```

Spam, spam, spam! Wonderful spam! Experiment joining with some other strings. The list `accumulator` could have been any list of strings.

Whatever string you use to join the elements of the list gets put in between each pair of elements.

Rewrite the Encryption Function

Now it's time to rewrite the encryption function:

1. Keep the same function name but update the function's docstring.

2. Change the function's definition to add an `encryption_dict` parameter.

```
def encrypt_msg(plaintext, encrypt_dict):
```

3. Comment out the old encryption code.

   You'll delete it when the new code is working.

4. Create an empty list to save up all the encrypted characters.

```
ciphertext = []
```

5. Iterate (go) through the plaintext and get the encrypted character by using the dictionary passed in.

```
for k in plaintext:
    v = encrypt_dict[k]
```

6. Store up the encrypted characters in your list.

```
ciphertext.append(v)
```

7. When it has made its way through the plaintext, join up the ciphertext and return it.

```
return ''.join(ciphertext)
```

8. Change the line where the function is called to add ENCRYPTION_DICT.

```
ciphertext = encrypt_msg(CHAR_SET, ENCRYPTION_DICT)
```

I commented out the old function and replaced it with this:

```
#### Function Section
def encrypt_msg(plaintext, encrypt_dict):
    """Take a plaintext message and encrypt each character using
    the encryption dictionary provided. key translates to its
    associated value.
    Return the cipher text"""
    ciphertext = []
    for k in plaintext:
        v = encrypt_dict[k]
        ciphertext.append(v)
        # you could just say
        # ciphertext.append(encrypt_dict[k])
        # I split it out so you could follow it better.
    return ''.join(ciphertext)
```

And in the Testing section I changed the line ciphertext = encrypt_msg(CHAR_SET) to ciphertext = encrypt_msg(CHAR_SET, ENCRYPTION_DICT):

```
ciphertext = encrypt_msg(CHAR_SET, ENCRYPTION_DICT)
```

Now run it:

```
>>> ================================ RESTART
================================
>>>
0123456789abcdefghijklmnopqrstuvwxyzABCDEFGHIJKLMNOPQRSTUVWXYZ
!"#$%&'()*+,-./:;<=>?@[\]^_`{|}~
}~ 0123456789abcdefghijklmnopqrstuvwxyzABCDEFGHIJKLMNOPQRSTUVW
XYZ!"#$%&'()*+,-./:;<=>?@[\]^_`{|
}~ 0123456789abcdefghijklmnopqrstuvwxyzABCDEFGHIJKLMNOPQRSTUVW
XYZ!"#$%&'()*+,-./:;<=>?@[\]^_`{|
```

When you're satisfied that the new code works, delete the code that's been commented out.

Write the Decryption Function

A coded message isn't going to do anyone any good if they can't decode it. You need some way to *decrypt* ciphertext. You can use the encryption structure to write a decryption function.

All you have to do is make a new copy of the `encrypt_msg` function and make these changes to the copy:

1. Rename it.

   ```
   def decrypt_msg(ciphertext, decrypt_dict):
   ```

2. Update the docstring.

3. Rename the `plaintext` argument to `ciphertext` (what you're decrypting) in three separate places.

   ```
   plaintext = []
       plaintext.append(v)
   return ''.join(plaintext)
   ```

4. Rename `encrypt_dict` to `decrypt_dict`.

   ```
   def decrypt_msg(ciphertext, decrypt_dict):
   ```

5. Create a decryption dictionary from the encryption dictionary.

   You do that in the next section.

6. Test the decryption function.

   You do that in the section after next.

The decryption function I get looks like this:

```
def decrypt_msg(ciphertext, decrypt_dict):
    """Take a ciphertext message and decrypt each character using
```

```
the decryption dictionary provided. key translates to its
associated value.
Return the plaintext"""
plaintext = []
for k in ciphertext:
    v = decrypt_dict[k]
    plaintext.append(v)
return ''.join(plaintext)
```

Create a decryption dictionary

To go from ciphertext to plaintext, you reverse what you did. For example, `'d'` encrypts to `'a'`, so `'a'` will decrypt to `'d'`. The encryption entry was `ENCRYPTION_DICT['d']= 'a'`. The matching decryption entry will be `DECRYPTION_DICT['a'] = 'd'`. You made the `ENCRYPTION_DICT` by assigning k→v.

You can make a decryption dictionary at the same time by doing the reverse assignment v→k. You can make the decryption dictionary by assigning `DECRYPTION_DICT[v]=k` in the loop you're using to create `ENCRYPTION_DICT`.

Here's the revised code to do this:

```
# generate encryption dictionary from the character set and
# its substitutions
ENCRYPTION_DICT = {}
DECRYPTION_DICT = {}
for i,k in enumerate(CHAR_SET):
    v = SUBSTITUTION_CHARS[i]
    ENCRYPTION_DICT[k]=v
    DECRYPTION_DICT[v]=k
```

Test the round trip

Now that you have your encryption and decryption functions working, test the *round trip*. That means encrypt a plaintext message to ciphertext and then decrypt it from ciphertext back to plaintext. Then compare them.

Follow these steps to test the decryption function:

1. Choose some plaintext to test. Save it as `test_message`.

   You've been using `CHAR_SET` so far. Test that first. Then you can use some more interesting plaintext.

   ```
   test_message = CHAR_SET
   ```

2. Print the `test_message`.

   ```
   print(test_message)
   ```

3. Encrypt the plaintext using `encrypt_msg`. Save it as `ciphertext`.

   ```
   ciphertext = encrypt_msg(test_message, ENCRYPTION_DICT)
   ```

4. Print the ciphertext.

   ```
   print(ciphertext)
   ```

5. Decrypt the ciphertext using `decrypt_msg`. Save that as `plaintext`.

   ```
   plaintext = decrypt_msg(ciphertext, DECRYPTION_DICT)
   ```

6. Print `plaintext`.

   ```
   print(plaintext)
   ```

7. Print the comparison `plaintext == test_message`.

   ```
   print(plaintext == test_message)
   ```

Did you end up with the same thing you started with?

I commented out some earlier `print` statements and got this:

```
#### Testing Section
##ciphertext = encrypt_msg(CHAR_SET, ENCRYPTION_DICT)
##print(CHAR_SET) # for comparison while testing
##print(ciphertext)
```

```
##print(SUBSTITUTION_CHARS) #what you should get
##print(ciphertext == SUBSTITUTION_CHARS) # are they the same?
##
##plaintext = decrypt_msg(ciphertext, DECRYPTION_DICT)
##print(plaintext)
##print(plaintext == CHAR_SET)

test_message = CHAR_SET
ciphertext = encrypt_msg(test_message, ENCRYPTION_DICT)
plaintext = decrypt_msg(ciphertext, DECRYPTION_DICT)

print(test_message)
print(ciphertext)
print(plaintext)
print(plaintext == test_message)
```

Running it should give you this:

```
>>> ================================ RESTART
================================
>>>
0123456789abcdefghijklmnopqrstuvwxyzABCDEFGHIJKLMNOPQRSTUVWXYZ
!"#$%&'()*+,-./:;<=>?@[\]^_`{|}~
}~ 0123456789abcdefghijklmnopqrstuvwxyzABCDEFGHIJKLMNOPQRSTUVW
XYZ!"#$%&'()*+,-./:;<=>?@[\]^_`{|
0123456789abcdefghijklmnopqrstuvwxyzABCDEFGHIJKLMNOPQRSTUVWXYZ
!"#$%&'()*+,-./:;<=>?@[\]^_`{|}~
True
```

You can compare the first line (test_message) to the third line (plaintext). However, the computer has done it for you in the last line. True means that these two lines are the same.

Try it with your own secret message. Change the value of test_message. Way back at the start of the project I suggested creating a constant called TEST_MESSAGE. You can use that now:

```
TEST_MESSAGE = "I like Monty Python.  They are very funny."
test_message = TEST_MESSAGE
```

You get this output:

```
>>> ================================= RESTART
=================================
>>>
I like Monty Python.  They are very funny.
F|ifhb|Jlkqv|Mvqelk+||Qebv|7ob|sbov|crkkv+
I like Monty Python.  They are very funny.
True
```

If you delete the code you commented out earlier, your code looks like this:

```python
"""Cryptopy
Take a plaintext message and encrypt it using a Caesar cipher
Brendan Scott, 2015
"""


#### Imports Section
import string


#### Constants Section
CHAR_SET = string.printable[:-5]
SUBSTITUTION_CHARS = CHAR_SET[-3:]+CHAR_SET[:-3]
# generate encryption dictionary from the character set and
# its substitutions
ENCRYPTION_DICT = {}
DECRYPTION_DICT = {}
for i,k in enumerate(CHAR_SET):
    v = SUBSTITUTION_CHARS[i]
    ENCRYPTION_DICT[k]=v
    DECRYPTION_DICT[v]=k



TEST_MESSAGE = "I like Monty Python.  They are very funny."

#### Function Section
def encrypt_msg(plaintext, encrypt_dict):
    """Take a plaintext message and encrypt each character using
    the encryption dictionary provided. key translates to its
```

```
        associated value.
        Return the cipher text"""
        ciphertext = []
        for k in plaintext:
            v = encrypt_dict[k]
            ciphertext.append(v)
            # you could just say
            # ciphertext.append(encrypt_dict[k])
            # I split it out so you could follow it better.
        return ''.join(ciphertext)


def decrypt_msg(ciphertext, decrypt_dict):
    """Take a ciphertext message and decrypt each character using
    the decryption dictionary provided. key translates to its
    associated value.
    Return the plaintext"""
        plaintext = []
        for k in ciphertext:
            v = decrypt_dict[k]
            plaintext.append(v)
        return ''.join(plaintext)



#### Testing Section
test_message = TEST_MESSAGE
ciphertext = encrypt_msg(test_message, ENCRYPTION_DICT)
plaintext = decrypt_msg(ciphertext, DECRYPTION_DICT)

print(test_message)
print(ciphertext)
print(plaintext)
print(plaintext == test_message)
```

Type in your plaintext or ciphertext

Now you need to apply the code to your own messages, rather
than hard coding the message you want to encrypt into the code.
(TEST_MESSAGE was hard coded.)

When data is typed into a program's code rather than coming from user input or another source, it's said to be *hard coded.*

The obvious way to get more messages to encrypt/decrypt is to use `raw_input`. Trouble, though: The program can encrypt and decrypt, but it can't tell whether it's getting plaintext to encrypt or ciphertext to decrypt.

You have ways around this, but the simplest is to just do both the encryption and the decryption! Users can choose the answer they want.

To do this:

1. Think of a prompt to use when asking for the message. The prompt should deal with both encryption and decryption and get a message to be handled with `raw_input`.

   ```
   message = raw_input("Type the message to encrypt below:\n")
   ```

2. Encrypt the message to ciphertext and decrypt the message to plaintext.

   ```
   ciphertext = encrypt_msg(message, ENCRYPTION_DICT)
   plaintext = decrypt_msg(message, DECRYPTION_DICT)
   ```

3. Print a short line saying `This message encrypts to`. Then print the ciphertext.

4. Print a short line saying `This message decrypts to`. Then print the plaintext.

   ```
   print("This message encrypts to")
   print(ciphertext)
   print  # just a blank line for readability
   print("This message decrypts to")
   print(plaintext)
   ```

I replaced the section marked `Testing Section` in the last full code readout with the following. (If you'd rather, you can comment out the code instead of deleting it.)

```
#### Input and Output Section
message = raw_input("Type the message to process below:\n")
ciphertext = encrypt_msg(message, ENCRYPTION_DICT)
plaintext = decrypt_msg(message, DECRYPTION_DICT)
print("This message encrypts to")
print(ciphertext)
print  # just a blank line for readability
print("This message decrypts to")
print(plaintext)
```

The \n character lets you type the message on a new line after the prompt. Running it gives you this:

```
>>> ================================ RESTART
================================
>>>
    Type the message you'd like to encrypt below:
I love learning Python. And my teacher is smelly.  And I shouldn't start
a sentence with and.
This message encrypts to
F|ilsb|ib7okfkd|Mvqelk+|xka|jv|qb79ebo|fp|pjbiiv+||xka|F|pelriak$q|pq7oq|
7|pbkqbk9b|tfqe|7ka+


This message decrypts to
L2oryh2ohduqlqj2SBwkrq;2Dqg2pB2whdfkhu2lv2vphooB;22Dqg2L2vkrxogq*w2vwduw2
d2vhqwhqfh2zlwk2dqg;
```

Run it again. This time, feed in the encrypted text to get the decryption. Copy and paste:

```
>>> ================================ RESTART
================================
>>>
    Type the message you'd like to encrypt below:
F|ilsb|ib7okfkd|Mvqelk+|xka|jv|qb79ebo|fp|pjbiiv+||xka|F|pelriak$q|pq7oq|
7|pbkqbk9b|tfqe|7ka+
```

```
This message encrypts to
C_fip8_f841hcha_Jsnbih(_uh7_gs_n846b81_cm_mg8ffs(__uh7_C_mbiof7h!n_
mn41n_4_m8hn8h68_qcnb_4h7(

This message decrypts to
I love learning Python. And my teacher is smelly.  And I shouldn't start
a sentence with and.
```

You'll get what you're looking for, but you'll have to print more information than you need. If this was a graphical interface (which you'll read about in the projects at dummies.com/go/pythonforkids), you could just have two separate buttons, one for encryption and one for decryption.

Encrypt a Text File

Having to type (or even copy and paste) your text into a `text_input` is a bit of a drag. One option is to have Python read the text from a file. This is pretty simple to do but the explanation is a little lengthy.

This only works for text (`.txt`) files — files that have no extra formatting or other instructions in them. If you try this on a word processing file (like `.docx` or `.doc`), you'll come to grief.

Open, write to, and close a file

Try this in the IDLE Shell window. Make sure you copy it exactly:

```
>>> file_object = open('p4k_test.py','w')
```

This tells Python to open a file on your computer's hard drive using the `open` built-in with the name `p4k_test.py` for writing, and to store the result in a variable called `file_object`. If a file called `p4k_test.py` already exists, this overwrites the file and deletes whatever was in it before.

If you ask Python to do something that will delete data, it will go ahead and do it. It *won't* warn you beforehand. It won't make a backup. Think twice before you do any file operations in Python. Do a test run if you're unsure.

Type `help(open)` at the interpreter to get the help text for open. It should tell you that it, "Open a file using the file() type, returns a file object.". That's why I called the variable `file_object` in the code. The file object isn't strictly speaking the file itself. You can think of it as an interface between the file and the rest of Python. That it's an object shouldn't be any surprise. You can use `dir` to find its attributes.

Type `dir(file_object)` now on the file object that you opened at the start of this section. You get a list of its attributes. Of these, `write`, `read`, `readlines`, and `close` are the ones you should pay attention to here.

When you finish with a file, you must call its `close` method.

Write something to the file and close it by creating a string (`text` in this example). Then use the `write` and `close` methods of the file object:

```
>>> text = "print('Hello from within the file')\n" # watch the " and '
>>> file_object.write(text) # writes it to the file
>>> file_object.write(text) # writes it to the file again!
>>> file_object.close() # finished with file, so close it
```

This stores a string in the variable `text`. The string ends in the new line character `\n`. It then writes this value to the file using the `write` method of `file_object`. (It writes it twice. I need the second line later to demonstrate something.) The `\n` character in the string puts each on a separate line. Then it closes the file.

Read the file

Open the file again — only this time use a `read` mode rather than a `write` mode.

If you open a file in write mode you destroy its contents. Make sure you copy this exactly. You have to change the 'w' (write) character to 'r' (read).

```
>>> file_object = open('p4k_test.py','r')
```

This line is only different from the earlier line by a single character — 'r' instead of 'w'. This opens the file in read mode (r for read? Brilliant!). Opening the file in read mode won't destroy the contents of the file. (Phew!)

When you've opened it, you can use the file_object read method:

```
>>> print(file_object.read())
print('Hello from within the file')
print('Hello from within the file')
```

The read method of file_object (which itself is an object of type file) reads the entire contents of the file. The file object also keeps track of how far through the file you've read and continues reading from where you left off. Since you've already read to the end of the file, you'll get nothing if you read again:

```
>>> print(file_object.read())
```

If you close the file and open it again, you can read from the start:

```
>>> file_object.close()
>>> file_object = open('p4k_test.py','r')
>>> print(file_object.read())
print('Hello from within the file')
print('Hello from within the file')

>>> file_object.close()   # finished, so close the file.
```

The readlines() method is, possibly, a more common way of reading from a file. Unlike read, which reads everything from the file's current position to the end, `readlines()` reads one line at a time.

```
>>> file_object.close()
>>> file_object = open('p4k_test.py','r')
>>> counter = 0
>>> for line in file_object.readlines():
        counter = counter +1
        print(str(counter)+ ": "+line)


1: print('Hello from within the file')

2: print('Hello from within the file')

>>> file_object.close()
```

The lines are separated from each other because each line in the file has a \n at the end of it, and the `print` statement is printing and then adding its own line break before the next line. You can verify that there is an \n at the end of each line because the variable `line` still has the last line of the file in it:

```
>>> line
"print('Hello from within the file')\n"
```

Run the file

The data you've written to the file is valid Python code. You can prove that the file that you've been writing to is an average, ordinary file (a Python file since you gave it a .py ending). You can run it: Open the file p4k_test.py with IDLE's Edit window. Run the file without making any changes to it.

```
>>> ==================================== RESTART
==================================
>>>
Hello from within the file
Hello from within the file
```

It's like you typed the code into the file directly.

Open and close with `with`

It's sometimes a pain to remember when to close a file that you've opened. Python has yet another keyword to deal with that (and other) issues — `with`. You put the `open` command after the `with` keyword, then you put an `as` keyword and the name of the dummy variable to hold the file object that will be created, like this:

```
>>> with open('p4k_test.py','r') as file_object:
        print(file_object.read())


print('Hello from within the file')
print('Hello from within the file')

>>> file_object
<closed file 'p4k_test.py', mode 'r' at 0xf7fed0>
```

Here Python opens the file named `p4k_test.py` in `read` mode and stores the object it creates in a variable named `file_object`. In the second line it reads and prints the contents of the file. When it gets to the end of the code block, Python realizes that you don't need the file anymore and cleans up after itself. (Do your parents wish you were a bit more like Python?) Part of this is that it closes the file. The last line tells you that the object is a closed file, so Python has closed the file for you.

You can use `with` for multiple files like this fake code. Don't type this at a command line. It won't work:

```
with open(filename1, 'r') as file_object1,
     open(filename2, 'r') as file_object2:
   do stuff with file_object1
   do stuff with file_object2
```

Fake code that shows the structure of real code is called *pseudocode*. (That's a silent p — psilly, I know.)

Here's a quick example in the Shell. This destroys any file called `testfile2`, so watch out!

```
>>> with open('testfile2','w') as a:
        a.write('stuff')


>>> with open('testfile2','r') as a,
         open('p4k_test.py','r') as b:
        print(a.read())
        print(b.read())


stuff
print('Hello from within the file')
print('Hello from within the file')

>>> a
<closed file 'testfile2', mode 'r' at 0xf6e540>
>>> b
<closed file 'p4k_test.py', mode 'r' at 0xef4ed0>
```

You'll mainly use the `with` keyword this way. From now on, use `with` unless you have a good reason not to.

Encrypt and Decrypt from a File

It's a bit of a hassle to cut and paste into the command line all the time. You're going to encrypt a file in the next two sections.

1. Choose a name for the file containing the plaintext to be encrypted (`cryptopy_input.txt`).

   Your application will be coded so that it only reads from this file and no others.

2. Create that file and put some test data in it.

3. Choose a name for the constant to use to store `cryptopy_input.txt` and set that constant.

   You can encrypt other files by changing this variable.

4. Choose a name for the file that will store the encrypted cipher-text (`cryptopy_output.txt`).

5. Choose a name for the constant to use to store `ciphertext.txt` and set that constant.

6. Open the input file.

7. Read the plaintext.

8. Close the input file.

9. Encrypt the file's contents.

10. Print the encrypted text.

    This is for the testing phase.

11. Open the output file.

12. Write the ciphertext.

13. Close the output file.

The process from Step 6 to Step 13 should replace the `Input` and `Output` section in the current version of the code, so delete (or comment out) that section and put this there.

Choose names and create the test data

The names I'm choosing for the input and output filenames are `INPUT_FILE_NAME` and `OUTPUT_FILE_NAME` respectively.

Use the Shell window to quickly create the input file and put some test data into it:

```
>>> INPUT_FILE_NAME = "cryptopy_input.txt"
>>> with open(INPUT_FILE_NAME,'w') as input_file:
        input_file.write('This is some test text')
```

You don't get any feedback on the file's creation, so if you're feeling suspicious, use your file explorer to check that the file really exists.

 The os.path library has a function — exists — that tells you whether a file exists. To use it, type import os.path, then call os.path.exists(<*path to file*>). Replace <*path to file*> with a string that has the relevant filename or a complete path to the file.

Open the file and encrypt the data

The main trick in opening a file is to tell the difference between the filename and the file object. The filename is what you give to the open built-in. The file object is what you get back from it. I use input_file and output_file to hold the file objects.

First add constants to hold the names of the input and output files to the Constants section. This is what I added:

```
INPUT_FILE_NAME = "cryptopy_input.txt"
OUTPUT_FILE_NAME = "cryptopy_output.txt"
```

Now do this:

1. Comment out the old Input and Output section.

2. In the Input and Output section, open the input file and read its contents into a variable called message.

```
with open(INPUT_FILE_NAME,'r') as input_file:
    message = input_file.read()
```

3. Use the `encrypt_msg` function to encrypt the message to ciphertext.

```
ciphertext = encrypt_msg(message, ENCRYPTION_DICT)
```

4. Open the output file and write the ciphertext to it.

```
with open(OUTPUT_FILE_NAME,'w') as output_file:
    output_file.write(ciphertext)
```

This is my finished code:

```
#### Input and Output Section
with open(INPUT_FILE_NAME,'r') as input_file:
    message = input_file.read()

ciphertext = encrypt_msg(message, ENCRYPTION_DICT)
print(ciphertext) # just for testing

with open(OUTPUT_FILE_NAME,'w') as output_file:
    output_file.write(ciphertext)
```

Pretty amazing that Steps 6 through 13 are all covered there, isn't it? Run it and you get this:

```
Qefp|fp|pljb|qbpq|qbuq
```

This pops up in the IDLE Shell window because of the `print` statement in the code. You can confirm it's been written to the file in IDLE's Shell window by opening the file and printing its contents, like this:

```
>>> OUTPUT_FILE_NAME = "cryptopy_output.txt"
>>> with open(OUTPUT_FILE_NAME,'r') as output_file:
        print(output_file.read())


Qefp|fp|pljb|qbpq|qbuq
```

Decrypt from Your Shell

It would be nice to decrypt this and test it in the interactive Shell without having to rerun the program (and write code to decrypt from a file). To do that you would need to somehow get the decrypt_msg function out of the cryptopy.py file and into the Shell. Luckily, you can use import to do this.

Go to your IDLE Shell window and type:

```
>>> import cryptopy
Qefp|fp|pljb|qbpq|qbuq
```

This is the same structure you used to import modules from the Python standard library. You can import any Python code. The only limit is that Python needs to be able to find that code. For you at the moment, that means that the code needs to be in C:\Python27. Now that you've imported this code, you can use the functions and constants defined within it.

Define a plaintext message:

```
>>> plaintext = """I wonder if I can use the functions and constants
from cryptopy to make encrypted messages from the command line?"""
```

Use the encrypt_msg function from the file. You need to treat cryptopy like the module name, just as if you had imported a module from the standard library:

```
>>> ciphertext = cryptopy.encrypt_msg(plaintext,cryptopy.
        ENCRYPTION_DICT)
```

Print it to see its encrypted stuff:

```
>>> ciphertext
'F|tlkabo|fc|F|97k|rpb|qeb|crk9qflkp|7ka|9lkpq7kqp|colj|9ovmqlmv\nql|
        j7hb|bk9ovmqba|jbpp7dbp|colj|qeb|9ljj7ka|ifkb<'
```

Now use the `decrypt_msg` function to decrypt it and confirm the round trip:

```
>>> print(cryptopy.decrypt_msg(ciphertext,cryptopy.DECRYPTION_DICT))
I wonder if I can use the functions and constants from cryptopy
to make encrypted messages from the command line?
```

Now you can pick the functions you want to use — even from the Python interpreter. You can use tab completion to get constant names like `cryptopy.ENCRYPTION_DICT` and so on. Just as you can use these functions within the interpreter, you can use them in a Python program, simply by importing the module.

There are some limits, though. To use the `import` statement, the module that you want to use must be either in one or the other:

✔ A directory listed in the `PYTHONPATH` environment variable.

✔ The current working directory of the Python script that's importing the file.

For now, put your application (and any modules it is to call) into `C:\Python27`.

When you imported cryptopy, some text printed: Qefp|fp|pljb|qbpq|qbuq. It looks a lot like some plaintext that's been encrypted. Try to decrypt it:

```
>>> ciphertext = "Qefp|fp|pljb|qbpq|qbuq"
>>> cryptopy.decrypt_msg(ciphertext,cryptopy.DECRYPTION_DICT)
'This is some test text'
```

This is the message you saved to `cryptopy_input.txt`. It's encrypted and printed out in the Input and Output section of cryptopy. When you imported cryptopy, Python needed to execute the whole file `cryptopy.py`, including the testing and input code. This is fine when you're running the module on its own, but you don't want that happening when other programs are importing the module. They just want access to the functions; they don't want the testing code run.

Python gives you a way to stop this code running when you import it. Python identifies the name of the code being run with a variable called __name__. (Remember *dunder name*?) When you run a file by itself, the value "__main__" ("dunder main") is assigned to this variable. Python automatically does this.

You can use the __name__ variable to identify whether the code is being run as an import. If __name__ is equal to "__main__", then the code isn't being imported. Otherwise, it is.

It's common in Python to isolate code (in an if block) that you don't want run during an import, like this:

```
>>> if __name__ == "__main__":
        print("Not in an import")


Not in an import
```

Tidy up the cryptopy script so it can be imported by other scripts:

1. Insert an if clause comparing __name__ to "__main__".

2. Move the existing code from the Input and Output section to the code block of that if clause.

The new Input and Output section looks like this. Notice the indented commented-out sections:

```
if __name__ == "__main__":
##      message = raw_input("Type the message to process below:\n")
##      ciphertext = encrypt_msg(message, ENCRYPTION_DICT)
##      plaintext = decrypt_msg(message, DECRYPTION_DICT)
##      print("This message encrypts to")
##      print(ciphertext)
##      print  # just a blank line for readability
##      print("This message decrypts to")
##      print(plaintext)
```

```
with open(INPUT_FILE_NAME,'r') as input_file:
    message = input_file.read()

ciphertext = encrypt_msg(message, ENCRYPTION_DICT)
print(ciphertext) # just for testing

with open(OUTPUT_FILE_NAME,'w') as output_file:
    output_file.write(ciphertext)
```

I will refer to this as the `Main` section in the rest of the book. Rename your `#### Input and Output Section` to `#### Main Section`.

Now when you import, Python loads the functions without running what was previously in the `Input and Output` section:

```
>>> import cryptopy # nothing should print
>>>
```

 This test `if __name__ == "__main__":` is a useful way to reuse the code you write without having to copy and paste it into your new files. Just import it.

This, in turn, means that instead of having one copy per file where it's used, one copy is imported. If the code has errors or features that ought to be added to the code, you can add them in (ideally) only one file. Other programs that rely on that code will automatically use the code that you updated.

Change the Code to Decrypt Too

At the moment, the code will only open a file and encrypt its contents. It would be useful if it could decrypt the contents. Should the code be encrypting or should it be decrypting when you run it?

You're going to deal with it by a switch in the software. Make a *switch* by setting a constant in the code and then executing one branch of code or another depending on how the switch is set.

To do so in this code, do the following in the Main section:

1. Name a constant.

   The constant will take either value True or the value False. If True, then it will encrypt the input file. If False, it will decrypt it. Create the constant and add it to the start of the Main section. (You could put it in the Constants section.)

   ```
   ENCRYPT = False # This is the constant used for the if
                   clause
   ```

2. Change all references from ciphertext to text_to_output.

   The name ciphertext is no longer accurate.

3. In between reading the input file and writing the output file, add an if clause.

   It tests this constant and encrypts or decrypts the contents of the input file depending on the value the switch takes.

   ```
   if ENCRYPT:
       text_to_output = encrypt_msg(message, ENCRYPTION_DICT)
   else:
       text_to_output = decrypt_msg(message, DECRYPTION_DICT)
   ```

The new Main section, excluding commented-out code, looks like this:

```
#### Main Section
if __name__ == "__main__":
    ENCRYPT = False # This is the constant used for the if clause

    with open(INPUT_FILE_NAME,'r') as input_file:
        message = input_file.read()
```

```
if ENCRYPT:
    text_to_output = encrypt_msg(message, ENCRYPTION_DICT)
else:
    text_to_output = decrypt_msg(message, DECRYPTION_DICT)

print(text_to_output) # just for testing

with open(OUTPUT_FILE_NAME,'w') as output_file:
    output_file.write(text_to_output)
```

I set the constant ENCRYPT to False (because the text is already encrypted). You can also see that, by choosing what code to change, you can easily decrypt.

To test the code, put some encrypted text in the input file. You can do that by writing the data there from the IDLE Shell window or by opening the file from within IDLE. Make sure you use the Files of Type drop-down menu on the Open dialog box to select Text Files (*.txt) or All Files (*). Otherwise, it won't show up in the window.

I cut and paste the earlier encrypted text in there:

```
Qefp|fp|pljb|qbpq|qbuq
```

This is what it looks like when you run it:

```
>>> ================================ RESTART
================================
>>>
This is some test text
```

A more common use of a switch of this kind is to have a constant called DEBUG (or similar) to turn on and off debugging-related code.

The Complete Code

My code ended up looking like this:

```python
"""Cryptopy
Take a plaintext message and encrypt it using a Caesar cipher
Take a ciphertext message and decrypt it using the same cipher
Encrypt/decrypt from and to a file
Brendan Scott, 2015
"""


#### Imports Section
import string

#### Constants Section
CHAR_SET = string.printable[:-5]
SUBSTITUTION_CHARS = CHAR_SET[-3:]+CHAR_SET[:-3]
# generate encryption dictionary from the character set and
# its substitutions
ENCRYPTION_DICT = {}
DECRYPTION_DICT = {}
for i,k in enumerate(CHAR_SET):
    v = SUBSTITUTION_CHARS[i]
    ENCRYPTION_DICT[k]=v
    DECRYPTION_DICT[v]=k
# other characters - \t, \n etc - are not changed
for c in string.printable[-5:]: # watch the colons!
    ENCRYPTION_DICT[c]=c
    DECRYPTION_DICT[c]=c

TEST_MESSAGE = "I like Monty Python.  They are very funny."
INPUT_FILE_NAME = "cryptopy_input.txt"
OUTPUT_FILE_NAME = "cryptopy_output.txt"

#### Function Section
def encrypt_msg(plaintext, encrypt_dict):
    """Take a plaintext message and encrypt each character using
```

```
        the encryption dictionary provided. key translates to its
        associated value.
    Return the cipher text"""
    ciphertext = []
    for k in plaintext:
        v = encrypt_dict[k]
        ciphertext.append(v)
        # you could just say
        # ciphertext.append(encrypt_dict[k])
        # I split it out so you could follow it better.
    return ''.join(ciphertext)


def decrypt_msg(ciphertext, decrypt_dict):
    """Take a ciphertext message and decrypt each character using
    the decryption dictionary provided. key translates to its
    associated value.
    Return the plaintext"""
    plaintext = []
    for k in ciphertext:
        v = decrypt_dict[k]
        plaintext.append(v)
    return ''.join(plaintext)



#### Main Section
if __name__ == "__main__":
##    message = raw_input("Type the message to process below:\n")
##    ciphertext = encrypt_msg(message, ENCRYPTION_DICT)
##    plaintext = decrypt_msg(message, DECRYPTION_DICT)
##    print("This message encrypts to")
##    print(ciphertext)
##    print  # just a blank line for readability
##    print("This message decrypts to")
##    print(plaintext)
```

```
ENCRYPT = False # This is the constant used for the if clause

with open(INPUT_FILE_NAME,'r') as input_file:
    message = input_file.read()

if ENCRYPT:
    text_to_output = encrypt_msg(message, ENCRYPTION_DICT)
else:
    text_to_output = decrypt_msg(message, DECRYPTION_DICT)

print(text_to_output) # just for testing

with open(OUTPUT_FILE_NAME,'w') as output_file:
    output_file.write(text_to_output)
```

Summary

In this project you read about:

🗸 A new data type — the dictionary. Dictionaries have items. Each item has a key and a value.

🗸 Dictionaries, which allow direct access to a value referenced by a key. If *key:value* is an item in the dictionary a_dictionary, the syntax to access the value is a_dictionary[key].

🗸 Creating empty dictionaries.

🗸 Creating items in existing dictionaries by creating *key:value* pairs in dictionaries and assigning values to keys.

🗸 Using Caesar ciphers.

🗸 Creating a string by joining a list together and using the join method.

🗸 Opening files on your computer using open and close.

✔ Reading from and writing to files on your computer using `read` and `write`.

✔ Using the `with` and `as` keywords to have Python clean up after you've used a file.

✔ Importing modules that aren't in the standard library. These could be your own modules or someone else's.

✔ Using `if __name__ == "__main__":` to isolate the functions in your file from the code being executed when the module is run separately.

✔ Using constants as switches to control program flow.

Silly Sentences

In this project you're going to put together a program that spits out a hilarious mixture of words — sort of like Mad Libs. To do this, you're going to tackle string formatting for prettier printing.

```
>>>
Tim sneezed the tired hovercraft.
Mrs Pepperpot sneezed the tight dinner.
Some dude threw the slimy hat.
Some dude wrote the tight walk.
Mrs Pepperpot sneezed the Python bag.
My Python teacher stole the big eels.
Dinsdale kissed the furry cat.
Mrs Pepperpot walked the heavy shoes.
Some dude cooked the tall joke.
My Python teacher wrote the silly shirt.
Mrs Pepperpot made the tall book.
Some dude ate the heavy coffee.
My Python teacher climbed the smelly hat.
Dinsdale lost the silly house.
Mrs Pepperpot cooked the funniest laptop.
My Python teacher drank the slippery laptop.
My dad cooked the silly drink.
Dinsdale stole the silly shirt.
A dog wrote the silly car.
A dog walked the heavy eels.
>>> |
```

This project's object is to create templates for words that are randomly chosen from a list. The randomness of the words makes them absurd and, hopefully, funny enough to make you laugh out loud.

To complete this project, you

1. Read about Python formatting strings.

2. Create templates for the formatting strings.

3. Create lists of words to put into the formatting strings.

4. Choose words at random.

5. Print the words into the template using formatting.

Insert Format Strings

Format strings let you fit changeable bits of a message into a template. That way it's easier to present your messages, and it makes your code more readable.

Fire up IDLE. At the interpreter, type the following and be careful — there are two strings. The first is `"Hi there %s. You are such a good author."` and the second is `"Brendan"`. In between them is the `%` character.

```
>>> print("Hi there %s. You are such a good author."%"Brendan")
Hi there Brendan.  You are such a good author.
```

Why, thank you. That's a very kind thing to say.

Can you see what has happened there? The second string (`"Brendan"`) was substituted into the first string in the place where the `%s` was.

In IDLE, the strings are in green and the % sign is black.

✔ The % sign is called Python's *formatting operator.*

✔ The string on the right of the % is the *formatting value.*

✔ The string on the left of the % is the *format string* (or *format template*).

✔ The first string's %s symbol is called a *conversion specifier.* (Seriously, I'm not making up these names.)

The specifier in this case (%s) says to convert the formatting value into a string. (s stands for string.) The main specifier you'll want is %s (that is, convert to a string). A lot of other specifiers exist, but you'll mainly work with these: integer %i, fixed point %f, general %g, and percent sign %.

Making messages according to a template is easier with formatting templates strings. For example, say you want to print out something like "You have 15 turns remaining until the end of the game." The number of turns keeps changing, but the rest of the message stays the same.

Have the Right Number of Values

To make a silly sentence, you need to mix up a heap of words into a message template. Substitute more than just one word into a template. To do that, follow these steps:

1. Include additional specifiers in the template.

2. List the values to be converted as if they were a list, but put parentheses around them instead of the square brackets used for a list.

3. Make sure the number of specifiers is equal to the number of values to be converted.

A quick example:

```
>>> "%s %s"%(1,2)
'1 2'
```

You get an error if the number of specifiers doesn't match the number of values to be formatted. Try these:

`"%s %s"%(1)`   (two specifiers, one value)

`"%s %s"%(1,2,3)`   (two specifiers, three values)

Pay attention to the errors; sooner or later you'll need them for debugging. You can pre-save your values before you pass them to your format string:

```
>>> values = (1,2)
>>> "%s %s"%values
'1 2'
>>> # Snuck in a tuple:
>>> type(values)
<type 'tuple'>
```

The formatting operator takes only one argument. When you place parentheses around a number of items separated by commas, you actually get a new object called a *tuple*. It is this single object that is passed to the formatting operator.

Tuh or tyoo

Debate rages over the correct pronunciation of tuple. I like it to rhyme with *supple,* even though it has only one *p.* It's easier to say and I think it sounds better. However, other people prefer *two-ple* or *tyoo-pull.* Please don't get into fisticuffs over it.

Use the Tuple Data Type

You'll have a couple of lists of words for the silly sentences. Choose one word from each list and put them together. The formatting operator only takes one argument, so pack all the words into an object so you can pass it, as a single argument, to the formatting operator. For that you need a tuple.

Tuples are the most misunderstood Python data type. They're a bit like lists. Some people think tuples are worse than lists, but they're just different. You can get the values of the elements of a tuple, but you can't change them. Tuples are *immutable,* which is a fancy way of saying you can't change them.

Tuples are good for

✏ When you have values that you want to put in a specific order. That's *exactly* what you want when you're using a format string.

✏ When you have a set of values that you don't want changed (either on purpose or by accident).

Tuple elements have a meaningful order. Lists are for things where order doesn't matter.

You can iterate (go) through tuples like you would a list and can read individual elements like a list:

```
>>> my_tuple = ('e','3')
>>> for e in my_tuple:
        print(e)


e
3
>>> my_tuple[0]
'e'
```

```
>>> my_tuple[1]
'3'
>>> my_tuple(0)  # use [] not ()!

Traceback (most recent call last):
  File "<pyshell#42>", line 1, in <module>
    my_tuple(0)  # [] not ()!
TypeError: 'tuple' object is not callable
```

Here, `my_tuple[0]` retrieves the value of the first element (elements are numbered from 0) in the tuple. It has the same square bracket notation that lists have. The number of the elements starts from 0, just like the substitutions were in the 133t sp34k3r project.

Confirm that you can't change the element by trying to assign a value to element 0: `my_tuple[0] = 17`. Be familiar with the error (it will tell you that tuples don't support item assignment) so you'll recognize it when you see it later.

You can have a tuple with only one element. Why? Because the code you want to use might expect a tuple. How would you make a tuple with only one element? The answer is to proceed as normal, putting parentheses around your one element, but to add a comma after it.

```
>>> my_one_element_tuple = (1,)
>>> my_one_element_tuple
(1,)
```

The comma tells Python that it's a tuple; technically it's the comma, not the parentheses, that's doing the work. You usually need to use parentheses because the syntax is hard to figure out.

Tuples let you return more than one value from a function, which is handy when you want to return more than one value from a function. But the code calling the function can treat the values as a single tuple or as individual elements. This is called *unpacking* the tuple.

You have to give the tuple exactly the right number of elements if you want the values unpacked. For example, here the test_function returns a tuple with three values (1,2,3). The code can either receive it as a single object a= test_function() or as three separate objects in a,b,c = test_function(), but not as any other number.

You can use this approach when you want to return more than one value from a function:

```
>>> def test_function():
        return (1,2,3)  # returns a tuple with three elements

>>> a = test_function()
>>> a
(1, 2, 3)
>>> a,b,c = test_function()
>>> a
1
>>> b
2
>>> c
3
>>> a,b = test_function()

Traceback (most recent call last):
  File "<pyshell#59>", line 1, in <module>
    a,b = test_function()
ValueError: too many values to unpack
```

You can also unpack a tuple directly:

```
>>> a,b,c = (1,2,3) # unpack the tuple into a, b, c
>>> print("a: %s, b: %s, c: %s"%(a,b,c))
a: 1, b: 2, c: 3
>>> a,b = (1,2,3) # three values but only two variables.

Traceback (most recent call last):
  File "<pyshell#62>", line 1, in <module>
    a,b = (1,2,3)
ValueError: too many values to unpack
```

Get Started on Your Silly Sentences

To make silly sentences, you need a template where you can plug in some words. Think of this like:

<Person or animal> <verbed> the <adjective> <noun>.

(Yeah, yeah. I know *verbed* isn't a word.) A formatting template for this would look like what you see here. Each `%s` is a conversion specifier and marks a place where a value will be inserted into the string:

```
template = "%s %s the %s %s."
```

Time to get started on your silly sentences:

1. Create a new file and name it `silly_sentencer.py`.

2. Add a comment at the top of the file that explains what the program will do.

```
"""silly_sentencer.py
This program prints silly sentences by mapping random words
into a formatting template
Brendan Scott
Jan 2015
"""
```

3. Create a template based on *<Person or animal> <verbed> the <adjective> <noun>*:

```
template = "%s %s the %s %s."
```

4. Store the following sample in a constant called BASE_SENTENCE.

   You'll look at this sentence when you're testing your code.

```
BASE_SENTENCE = "My Python teacher wrote the Python book."
```

5. Type the following into your code:

```
persons = ["My Python teacher"]
verbs = ["wrote"]
adjectives = ["Python"]
nouns = ["book"]
```

When you're first working on a project, start simple. Make it more complex later. Don't try to conquer the universe in your first go. That way, miMMisMistakes are easier to find and fix.

You should have something that looks like this:

```
"""silly_sentencer.py
This program prints silly sentences by mapping random words
into a formatting template
Brendan Scott
Jan 2015
"""

BASE_SENTENCE = "My Python teacher wrote the Python book."
template = "%s %s the %s %s."

persons = ["My Python teacher"]
verbs = ["wrote"]
adjectives = ["Python"]
nouns = ["book"]
```

Now test to make sure that applying the values from the lists to the template gives you the base sentence.

1. Create a Main section.

2. Add the following code and run the file.

This code creates a tuple from the first element of each list, then passes that tuple into the formatting string. The last `print` statement compares whether the formatted string is the same as what you started with:

```
# Main Section
if __name__ == "__main__":
    person = persons[0]
    verb = verbs[0]
    adjective = adjectives[0]
    noun = nouns[0]

    format_values = (person, verb, adjective, noun)

    print(BASE_SENTENCE)
    print(template%format_values)
    print(BASE_SENTENCE == template%format_values)
```

You should get this:

```
>>> ================================ RESTART
================================
>>>
My Python teacher wrote the Python book.
My Python teacher wrote the Python book.
True
```

Spam

Spam is a brand of meat in a can. Spam also is the centerpiece of a ridiculous skit by Monty Python. In it, a man and woman want to get something to eat at a small café. The woman doesn't like Spam, but everything on the menu has Spam in it.

The Vikings are sitting at another table (yes, Vikings) and start singing a song about how great Spam is. This skit is the reason dummy variables in Python are sometimes called *spam* (also *ham and eggs*). It's also why the email that you don't want is called *spam.*

Fill the Template

To fill in the template, choose an element from each list at random. Because there's only one element in each list at the moment, it's not all that random. However, you're testing with one element and then adding other elements later. When you have that, you can use the code you already have to populate the template with the words you've chosen.

Choosing at random from a list is relatively easy. Use the `choice` function from the `random` module. In this example I use a list comprehension to make a list with the numbers from 0 through 9, then I use `random.choice` to choose one of them at random:

```
>>> import random
>>> sample_list = [x for x in range(10)]
>>> random.choice(sample_list)
1
```

Now bring it all together in your code:

1. Remove, or comment out, the `print` statements and other code included for testing.

2. Replace each assignment like `person = persons[0]` with something like `person = random.choice(persons)`.

3. Make a tuple with the format values.

4. Print out the base sentence for comparison and the template formatted with the format values.

    Here's the code:

    ```
    """silly_sentencer.py
    This program prints silly sentences by mapping random words
    into a formatting template
    Brendan Scott
    Jan 2015
    """
    ```

```
# Imports Section
import random

# Constants Section
BASE_SENTENCE= "My Python teacher wrote the Python book."
template = "%s %s the %s %s."

persons = ["My Python teacher"]
verbs = ["wrote"]
adjectives = ["Python"]
nouns = ["book"]


# Main Section
if __name__ == "__main__":
    person = random.choice(persons)
    verb = random.choice(verbs)
    adjective = random.choice(adjectives)
    noun = random.choice(nouns)

    format_values = (person, verb, adjective, noun)

    print(BASE_SENTENCE)
    print(template%format_values)
```

5. Run it!

You're testing that the function works properly.

```
>>> ================================= RESTART
=================================
>>>
My Python teacher wrote the Python book.
My Python teacher wrote the Python book.
```

This code looks like it's working right. The first line is the original string you started with. The second is the string you created using the formatting template.

Add More Words

Now you can get creative. For each list think of other words which you could put in there. You haven't tested your code with a list longer than one yet, so just add words to a single list, not all of them at once.

The other words that you're choosing:

✔ Must be the same type as the original word. For example, for persons you might add *The Hungarian* and for adjectives you might add *slippery,* but you wouldn't do the reverse. Otherwise, the sentence wouldn't make any sense: "slippery was The Hungarian."

✔ Should be single words. They can be multiples. For example, *Mrs Pepperpot* or *The Hungarian.*

✔ Shouldn't be pronouns: *he, she, it, we, us, they.* You'd need to match the pronoun to the gender.

Here are some extra words to get you started:

```
persons = ["My Python teacher", "Dinsdale Piranha", "Tim", "Mrs
            Pepperpot", "My dad", "The Hungarian"]
verbs = ["wrote", "sneezed", "looked at", "drove", "made", "stole"]
adjectives = ["Python", "slippery", "funniest", "big", "smelly",
            "poky", "silly"]
nouns = ["book", "eels", "hovercraft", "nose", "shoes", "joke",
            "walk"]
```

You can split a long list

over multiple lines. (Like that.)

You can add a new line after any comma.

When you've got all the elements you want, finish with a closing square bracket (and no comma). Run the code a few times to see if it works. (I removed the restart lines from this printout.)

```
Mrs Pepperpot looked at the big eels.
My dad sneezed the funniest shoes.
Dinsdale Piranha wrote the Python book.
Dinsdale Piranha wrote the silly nose.
Tim made the Python shoes.
My dad made the Python walk.
My Python teacher drove the slippery joke.
Tim wrote the Python shoes.
```

Everything seems to be working. This function is a little hard to test because the output is random (unlike addition, where you know what the answer should be).

When you're satisfied, you can finish filling out your word lists. If you like, you can also put the whole section into a `for` loop to print multiple sentences each time you run the program.

The Complete Code

If you add those changes to the previous code, you get your final code. It looks like this:

```
"""silly_sentencer.py
This program prints silly sentences by mapping random words
into a formatting template
Brendan Scott
Jan 2015
"""


# Imports Section
import random


# Constants Section
BASE_SENTENCE = "My Python teacher wrote the Python book."
template = "%s %s the %s %s."
```

```
persons = ["My Python teacher", "Dinsdale Piranha", "Tim", "Mrs
                Pepperpot", "My dad", "The Hungarian"]
verbs = ["wrote", "sneezed", "looked at", "drove", "made", "stole"]
adjectives = ["Python", "slippery", "funniest", "big", "smelly",
                "poky", "silly"]
nouns = ["book", "eels", "hovercraft", "nose", "shoes", "joke",
                "walk"]


# Main Section
if __name__ == "__main__":
    person = random.choice(persons)
    verb = random.choice(verbs)
    adjective = random.choice(adjectives)
    noun = random.choice(nouns)

    format_values = (person, verb, adjective, noun)

##    print(BASE_SENTENCE)
    print(template%format_values)
```

Summary

In this project you used Python's formatting operator % to produce silly sentences. Along the way you saw:

- Format strings, a formatting operator, a formatting value, and conversion specifiers.

- The string conversion specifier: %s.

- A new data type — the *immutable* (can't be changed) tuple.

- That tuples store elements with a meaningful order, can return multiple values from a function, and can be unpacked: a, b = (1,2).

- The random.choice function and how to use it to get an element at random from a list.

Week 4
Stepping Up to Object-Oriented Programming

```
*Python 2.7.9 Shell*                                                    _ □ X

File  Edit  Shell  Debug  Options  Windows  Help

Python 2.7.9 (default, Dec 10 2014, 12:24:55) [MSC v.1500 32 bit (Intel)] on win
32
Type "copyright", "credits" or "license()" for more information.
>>> ============================ RESTART ============================
>>>
Address Book Application (Python for Kids for Dummies)
Press:
a to add an entry
d to display a list of all entries in summary form.
i to print these instructions again
The entry's number to show the secret note for that entry.
q to quit.

What would you like to do? d
Displaying Summaries
1: Name: Eric Idle      Born: March 29, 1943. Next birthday: 13 days
2: Name: John Cleese      Born: October 27, 1939. Next birthday: 225 days
3: Name: Graham Chapman      Born: January 8, 1941. Next birthday: 298 days
What would you like to do? 1
Decrypting record number 1
What is the secret passphrase? Wow! This is a great book.
Secret note is:
I think the Eric IDE was named after him.

What would you like to do? 1
Decrypting record number 1
What is the secret passphrase? don't know
Secret note is:
F|qefkh|qeb|Bof9|FAB|t7p|k7jba|7cqbo|efj+|
```

This week you're building an . . .

Address Book

In this project you create a basic address book in which you can store your friend's name, email address, and birthday. Or you can store your friends' names, email addresses, and birthdays. You know. Some people like to keep a tight circle. You could extend the address book to include anything else about them. Did they borrow your favorite book or a dollar for lunch?

```
Python 2.7.9 (default, Dec 10 2014, 12:24:55) [MSC v.1500 32 bit (Intel)] on win
32
Type "copyright", "credits" or "license()" for more information.
>>> ============================== RESTART ==============================
>>>
Address Book Application (Python for Kids for Dummies)
Press:
a to add an entry
d to display a list of all entries in summary form.
i to print these instructions again
The entry's number to show the secret note for that entry.
q to quit.

What would you like to do? d
Displaying Summaries
1: Name: Eric Idle    Born: March 29, 1943. Next birthday: 13 days
2: Name: John Cleese    Born: October 27, 1939. Next birthday: 225 days
3: Name: Graham Chapman    Born: January 8, 1941. Next birthday: 298 days
What would you like to do? 1
Decrypting record number 1
What is the secret passphrase? Wow! This is a great book.
Secret note is:
I think the Eric IDE was named after him.

What would you like to do? 1
Decrypting record number 1
What is the secret passphrase? don't know
Secret note is:
F|qefkh|qeb|Bof9|FAB|t7p|k7jba|7cqbo|efj+|

What would you like to do? |
```

To put the address book together, you make your own objects, called *classes*. These custom (made-by-you) objects are the spine of Python work. In this project, you also see how to store your data in files so you can load your info later.

Your First Class Objects

Address books have a lot of individual entries. The structure of each entry is pretty much the same, although the names are changed (to protect the innocent). You're going to create your own personalized Python objects (called *classes*) to reuse for each address book entry by using Python's `class` keyword.

Classes are a part of *object-oriented programming (OOP)*. OOP groups data with their related functions.

You need to know about *custom objects* (objects you make yourself) to understand the projects at `dummies.com/go/pythonforkids`.

Earlier when you created a string, Python packed up a heap of string methods for you. When you wrote a function, Python got the docstring for the help facility for you. You're going to have to get your hands dirty now, by making your own classes and squishing around their internals. (Eeew!)

Python objects have two parts:

- A *class declaration,* which helps you create the objects themselves. (Each is called an *instance* of the class.) Creating an instance is called *instantiation*. Classes are like a factory for creating instances. The instances are nearly copies of their corresponding class, but they're not clones because you don't use them to make more copies.

- *Instances* of the class declaration. You use classes like a mold to create the instances. When you use a class declaration, the object you create (*instantiate* is the computer term) is called an *instance* of the class.

Create a Class

The address book project uses two classes:

✔ One for the address book. It will only have one instance.

✔ One for the address entries. It will have one instance for each person whose details you store.

Creating a class is a little like creating a function:

1. Name the class.

   Use an initial capital (per PEP8). If the name has two or more words, use CapsWords to show the new word. (Don't insert spaces between words, but do capitalize the first letter in each new word.)

2. Type this:

   ```
   class <the class name you've chosen>(object):
   ```

   The '(object)' bit means that this class is a kind of object. It is said to *inherit from* object. Class inheritance is important, but you don't need to know the details right now. Unless I say otherwise, include the '(object)' bit in all your class statements.

3. Add a docstring explaining the purpose of the class.

   The docstring starts a new code block, so indent it.

4. Go down a line, indent, and put the stuff that makes up the class in a new code block on the next line.

   For now, put a pass keyword (technically not necessary since you have a docstring).

You'll use this a stub for the AddressEntry class later. Work in the IDLE Shell window for the time being so you can interact directly with the instances:

```
>>> class AddressEntry(object):
    """

    AddressEntry instances hold and manage details of a person

    """

    pass

>>> AddressEntry # without parentheses
<class '__main__.AddressEntry'>
>>>
```

When you press Return twice after the `pass` statement, the class is created. If you type the name of the class without parentheses, Python says (in the readout) that there's a class, which is part of __main__ with the name AddressEntry.

Create an Instance

You create instances of a class by adding parentheses after the name of the class (like the class was a function). This creates an instance of the `AddressEntry` class, but doesn't store it:

```
>>> AddressEntry() # parentheses create an instance
<__main__.AddressEntry object at 0x7f9309751590>
```

Normally though, you'd choose a variable name to hold the class instance and assign the instance to the variable like this:

```
>>> address_entry = AddressEntry()
```

Notice the different naming convention for the instance:

✔ On the left, lowercase_words are separated by an underscore.

✔ On the right, CapsWords with no separations.

Using lowercase for instances and CapsWords for classes helps you tell the difference between classes (`AddressEntry`) and class instances (`address_entry`).

Notice also that Python's description of the object is different:

```
AddressEntry: <class '__main__.AddressEntry'>

address_entry: <__main__.AddressEntry object at 0x7f9309751590>
```

Do a `dir` listing for each object to see its base attributes.

Create Class and Instance Attributes

In other projects, I ask you to find out about objects' attributes. Your custom classes should have attributes, too.

You can create attributes of class definitions or instances by using the dot syntax you've been using for object methods. For example, in Project 6 you use `my_message.upper()` to access the `upper` method of the `my_message` object. You use this dot syntax to assign a value to the attribute with your desired name.

Here's an example where attributes called `class_attribute` and `instance_attribute` are created and a string assigned to each one, in order:

```
>>> AddressEntry.class_attribute = "This is a class attribute"
>>> address_entry.instance_attribute = "This is an instance attribute"
>>> AddressEntry.class_attribute
'This is a class attribute'
>>> address_entry.instance_attribute
'This is an instance attribute'
```

Now here's a surprise for you:

```
>>> address_entry.class_attribute
'This is a class attribute'
```

The instance has inherited the class's attribute — even though the instance *already existed* (you created it in the previous section) when the attribute was created. However, the class didn't inherit the instance attribute. (Use `dir` to check if you don't believe me.)

When Python accesses attributes, it looks them up in a specific order at the time you need them. This is why the instance inherits new attributes of the class, even after the instance was created, but the class doesn't inherit new attributes of the instance. I don't expect this to make sense right now, but it will later.

You'll often want to create a class with default values for the attributes that instances will need. However, those values are just defaults. You usually want to change them later (less often for methods, but you'll get an example of a method to be changed later).

Create a new instance (`address_entry2`) and change the attribute named `class_attribute`.

When an instance assigns a new value to an attribute that the class has, the instance is said to *override* that attribute of the class:

```
>>> address_entry2 = AddressEntry()
>>> address_entry2.class_attribute = "An overridden class attribute"
>>> address_entry2.class_attribute
'An overridden class attribute'
>>> AddressEntry.class_attribute
'This is a class attribute'
```

It only overrides the attribute in that instance. The class and other instances don't have that attribute changed.

Plan Your Address Book

Your address book will store these tidbits:

✔ First name

✔ Last name

✔ Email address

✔ Birthday

You can also add other entries like private notes about them, kik, Skype, and Twitter accounts, who they're friends with, and who they're related to.

Set Up Your File and Create a Class

Things to do at this step are:

1. Create a new file!

   Ah, yeah. Sorry. Gotta tell you every time. How about you call it `address_book.py`?

2. Write a module docstring telling the world that this is an address book application.

3. Add a `#### Classes` section.

4. In the `Classes` section, create and name a class stub `AddressBook`.

   The stub will store the address book. Make sure you remember a docstring.

   You create a stub for a class pretty much the same way you do for a function. Use the `AddressEntry` code, but change the name and docstring.

5. In the `Classes` section, copy in the code for `AddressEntry`.

6. Create a `##### Main` section.

7. In the `Main` section, create a main block and instantiate one instance of each class.

   Choose a name for a variable to store each.

Did you get something like this?

```
"""
Addressbook.py
An address book program to store details of people I know.
Stuff I'm storing is:
first name
family name
email address
date of birth
[other stuff]

Brendan Scott
Feb 2015

"""


##### Classes Section
class AddressBook(object):
    """
    AddressBook instances hold and manage a list of people
    """
    pass

class AddressEntry(object):
    """
    AddressEntry instances hold and manage details of a person
    """

##### Main Section

if __name__ == "__main__":
    address_book = AddressBook()
    person1 = AddressEntry()
```

When run, you shouldn't see any output (no news is good news), but it will create the classes and create an instance of each class.

Add Your First Person

You can create attributes and values for an instance by assigning them as you would for any object.

For example, you could create an entry for a person like this. This continues from where you left off in the IDLE Shell window:

```
>>> person1 = AddressEntry()# creates the entry
>>> person1.first_name = "Eric" # sets the first name etc.
>>> person1.family_name = "Idle"
>>> person1.date_of_birth = "March 29, 1943"
>>> person1.email_address = None
```

Python gives you a way of streamlining the initialization of an instance's values at the time of the creation of the instance. Create a method in the class named __init__. This method is called whenever an instance is created, so it can initialize values for the instance.

For historical reasons, __init__ is called a *constructor* method instead of an initializer. In object-oriented programming, constructors are functions that prepare a new object for use.

As you know, a method is a function which is part of an object. To make an __init__ method for one of your custom classes, you define a function called __init__ within the code block of the class.

Here's what you need to know:

✔ You don't need to think of a name. It's __init__. You've got no choice.

✔ Unlike normal functions, all methods need to be defined with at least one argument. That first argument is always called self. If you want to initialize attributes with values — that is, when you instantiate the class you want to configure some initial values — pass in the values as arguments and assign them to attributes.

Here's example code for the `AddressEntry` class. The main things to initialize when you're creating an instance are the person's first and last name, email address, and birthdate. So you add a dummy argument for each one in the definition statement:

```
class AddressEntry(object):
    """
    AddressEntry instances hold and manage details of a person
    """
    def __init__(self, first_name=None, family_name=None,
                 email_address=None, date_of_birth=None):
        """Initialize attributes first_name,
        family_name and date_of_birth.
        Each argument should be a string.
        date_of_birth should be of the form "MM DD, YYYY"
        """
        self.first_name = first_name
        self.family_name = family_name
        self.email_address = email_address
        self.date_of_birth = date_of_birth
```

Define the `__init__` method by using a `def` statement. It has an argument list just like you'd expect for a function. The arguments here are taking default values (except for `self` — you and I talk about your sense of `self` in a moment).

Please pay attention to the indentation. The `__init__` method is part of the class's code block, so everything in it is one indent to the right more than it would be if it were defined as a function.

I added a docstring here because you're supposed to. Sometimes I'm naughty and leave out the docstring for `__init__`.

The method doesn't have a `return` statement at the end. You don't need one. In this case, lots of assignments are made to attributes of the object `self` (that is, the first argument that was passed to the method). Think back for a moment to the previous

Use `self`

Using the name `self` for receiving a reference to the instance of the object is just a convention. It's possible to use a different name, but don't. Using `self` makes your code consistent with other people's. Also, your Python friends won't invite you to parties if you call it something else.

section. There you created an attribute called `first_name` by doing this: `person1.first_name = "Eric"`. When you're writing the constructor (`__init__`), it's part of the class definition. That's written before any instances are created.

You can't use the name of an instance to create an attribute in `__init__`. What's more, you can't choose the name of any particular instance because it'll be wrong for every other instance. That's where the magic of `self` comes in.

When you make any method of a class, Python reserves the first argument to be a copy of itself. That way, you don't need to know the name of the instance. All you need to know is the name of the dummy variable used to reference it. In this case, that name is `self`. At the time you instantiate an instance, a reference to that instance is passed to `__init__`.

Instantiate an Instance Using `__init__`

Time to actually use this newfangled code to create an instance:

1. Update your `AddressEntry` class to include the code for `__init__`.

2. In the `Main` section, create a new instance like this:

```
person1 = AddressEntry("Eric", "Idle", None, "March 29, 1943")
```

3. Add a line to print out `person1` to the `Main` section.

Your code for the `Classes` section and `Main` section should look like this:

```
##### Classes Section
class AddressBook(object):
    """
    AddressBook instances hold and manage a list of people
    """
    pass


class AddressEntry(object):
    """
    AddressEntry instances hold and manage details of a person
    """
    def __init__(self, first_name=None, family_name=None,
                 email_address=None, date_of_birth=None):
        """Initialize attributes first_name,
        family_name and date_of_birth.
        Each argument should be a string.
        date_of_birth should be of the form "MM DD, YYYY"
        """
        self.first_name = first_name
        self.family_name = family_name
        self.email_address = email_address
        self.date_of_birth = date_of_birth


##### Main Section

if __name__ == "__main__":
    address_book = AddressBook()
    person1 = AddressEntry("Eric", "Idle", None, "March 29, 1943")
    print(person1)
```

Running this code should get you output that looks something along the lines of `<__main__.AddressEntry object at`

0x7f6225c9cc10> or something equally unglamorous. That's because Python has no idea how to print your custom object. It can't tell what data in the object is important to print and what isn't, whether you want everything printed or just a summary, and yadda. It takes the easy way out and prints the kind of object it is and where it's stored in memory.

How can you tell whether the initialization worked? Right now you can't. Printing out the details of an AddressEntry instance is the next problem you solve.

Create a Function to Print the Instance

You need a function that prints out details of an AddressEntry instance. Then you'll be able to check whether your initialization worked properly.

To do this, follow the steps:

1. Add a ##### Functions section before the ##### Main section.

2. Create a function, called __repr__, that takes a single argument.

   That argument will be an instance of AddressEntry and will print out its attributes. Call that argument self for now. Can you guess why you're calling it self? (Hint: It's a method later.)

3. In the function, use %s formatting specifiers to create a template that looks like this:

```
template = "AddressEntry(first_name='%s', "+\
            "family_name='%s',"+\
            " email_address='%s', "+\
            "date_of_birth='%s')"
```

4. Return the template filled with the corresponding attributes from the `AddressEntry` by making a tuple (`self.first_ name, self.family_name, self.email_address, self.date_of_birth`).

Format it with the template.

5. Add a line to `print(__repr__(person1))` in the `Main` section.

The `Classes` section doesn't change. For the new `Functions` and `Main` sections you should get this:

```
##### Functions Section
def __repr__(self):
    """
    Given an AddressEntry object self return
    a readable string representation
    """
    template = "AddressEntry(first_name='%s', "+\
               "family_name='%s',"+\
               " email_address='%s', "+\
               "date_of_birth='%s')"
    return template%(self.first_name, self.family_name,
                    self.email_address, self.date_of_birth)


##### Main Section

if __name__ == "__main__":
    address_book = AddressBook()
    person1 = AddressEntry("Eric", "Idle", None, "March 29, 1943")
    print(person1)
    print(__repr__(person1))
```

When you run this code, you will get a printout that looks like this:

```
<__main__.AddressEntry object at 0x2772d50>
AddressEntry(first_name='Eric', family_name='Idle',
email_address='None', date_of_birth='March 29, 1943')
```

The first line is the output of print(person1). The second line is from the new __repr__ function. Notice two things:

✔ Each attribute is correct (technically, 'None' should be None without the quotes, but it was going to be a little too involved to do that properly). This means that your __init__ function is properly initializing the attributes.

✔ The output (apart from None) is good enough to copy and paste into your code to create a new AddressEntry.

Use __repr__ Magic

Did you figure out why you used the name self? Back in Project 4 (remember that long ago?) I told you that functions that start with __ have a special meaning in Python; __repr__ is one of them.

Whenever Python prints an object it calls the object's __repr__ method.

If you do a dir listing on one of your AddressEntry instances you will see it has a __repr__ method already. It's that __repr__ method that is printing out <__main__.AddressEntry object at 0x2772d50>. If you override this method, the function you've just created will be called whenever you call print.

To do it quickly, add this line at the end of your Functions section, just before your Main section. Why aren't there parentheses here?

```
AddressEntry.__repr__ = __repr__
```

Then run the code again. You get this:

```
AddressEntry(first_name='Eric', family_name='Idle',
email_address='None', date_of_birth='March 29, 1943')
AddressEntry(first_name='Eric', family_name='Idle',
email_address='None', date_of_birth='March 29, 1943')
```

Is that magic? It's magic isn't it? Go on, you know it is.

The code AddressEntry.__repr__ = __repr__ substitutes your newly written __repr__ function for the default __repr__ method that Python gave to your class when you created it. (It got that method from the object class it inherited from.) Now that you made this substitution to print an instance like person1, all you need to do is type print(person1).

The code AddressEntry.__repr__ = __repr__ was a patch job. The proper thing to do is move the __repr__ code into the class definition as a new method:

1. Cut and paste the code of the __repr__ function into AddressEntry below the __init__ method. Then indent it one level.

2. Delete the code AddressEntry.__repr__ = __repr__.

   Your Functions section should be empty.

3. Delete the line print(__repr__(person1)).

   You don't need it, and it won't work now that you've moved __repr__.

Here's the new code for the AddressEntry class and the Functions (empty) and Main sections:

```
class AddressEntry(object):
    """
    AddressEntry instances hold and manage details of a person
    """
    def __init__(self, first_name=None, family_name=None,
                 email_address=None, date_of_birth=None):
        """initialize attributes first_name, family_name
           and date_of_birth
        each argument should be a string
        date_of_birth should be of the form "MM DD, YYYY"
        """
```

```
            self.first_name = first_name
            self.family_name = family_name
            self.email_address = email_address
            self.date_of_birth = date_of_birth

    def __repr__(self):
        """
        Given an AddressEntry object self return
        a readable string representation
        """
        template = "AddressEntry(first_name='%s', "+\
                   "family_name='%s',"+\
                   " email_address='%s', "+\
                   "date_of_birth='%s')"
        return template%(self.first_name, self.family_name,
                         self.email_address, self.date_of_birth)


##### Functions Section


##### Main Section

if __name__ == "__main__":
    address_book = AddressBook()
    person1 = AddressEntry("Eric", "Idle", None, "March 29, 1943")
    print(person1)
```

Initialize the `AddressBook` Instance

At the moment, your AddressBook class is only a placeholder. It's supposed to store a list of people. Time for AddressBook to pull its weight. You also include a way to add AddressEntry instances to that list:

1. Delete the pass statement in the AddressBook class.

2. Create a skeleton __init__ method.

   It only needs self as an argument.

3. Write a docstring.

4. Set the attribute `people` to be an empty list.

5. Create a method called `add_entry` in the `AddressBook` class.

6. Define it to have two arguments — `self` and `new_entry`.

7. Write a docstring for it. It's adding `new_entry` to the list `people`.

8. Use `self.people.append(new_entry)` to add the entry.

9. In the `Main` section, add `address_book.add_entry` `(person1)`. Then add `print(address_book.people)`.

The `AddressEntry` code hasn't changed. The code right now, including the new `AddressBook` code and the `Main` section, is this:

```
"""
Addressbook.py
An address book program to store details of people I know.
Stuff I'm storing is:
first name
family name
email address
date of birth
[other stuff]

Brendan Scott
Feb 2015

"""


##### Classes Section
class AddressBook(object):
    """
    AddressBook instances hold and manage a list of people
    """
```

```python
    def __init__(self):
        """ Set people attribute to an empty list"""
        self.people = []

    def add_entry(self, new_entry):
        """ Add a new entry to the list of people in the
        address book the new_entry should be an instance
        of the AddressEntry class"""
        self.people.append(new_entry)

class AddressEntry(object):
    """
    AddressEntry instances hold and manage details of a person
    """
    def __init__(self, first_name=None, family_name=None,
                 email_address=None, date_of_birth=None):
        """Initialize attributes first_name,
        family_name and date_of_birth.
        Each argument should be a string.
        date_of_birth should be of the form "MM DD, YYYY"
        """
        self.first_name = first_name
        self.family_name = family_name
        self.email_address = email_address
        self.date_of_birth = date_of_birth

    def __repr__(self):
        """
        Given an AddressEntry object self return
        a readable string representation
        """
        template = "AddressEntry(first_name='%s', "+\
                "family_name='%s',"+\
                " email_address='%s', "+\
                "date_of_birth='%s')"
        return template%(self.first_name, self.family_name,
                    self.email_address, self.date_of_birth)
```

```
##### Functions Section

##### Main Section

if __name__ == "__main__":
    address_book = AddressBook()
    person1 = AddressEntry("Eric", "Idle", None, "March 29, 1943")
    print(person1)
    address_book.add_entry(person1)
    print(address_book.people)
```

When you run this, you get:

```
AddressEntry(first_name='Eric', family_name='Idle',
email_address='None', date_of_birth='March 29, 1943')
[AddressEntry(first_name='Eric', family_name='Idle',
email_address='None', date_of_birth='March 29, 1943')]
```

The second line is the list `people` (notice the `[]`), which has one entry — `person1`. Python has been working magic again here. It called `__repr__` when it printed out `person1`. You could, if you wanted to, create a `__repr__` method for `AddressBook`, but it's not necessary.

Find Pickle Power

To save your address book, you need to write its contents out to a file. Here's where the power of pickles comes in! (In the background, a hapless victim calls out, "Save me with the power of a pickle!")

Import the `pickle` module and use its `dump` method. It needs an open file. (Go back to Project 7 if you forgot how to open files.)

Here's an example:

```
>>> import pickle
>>> FILENAME = "p4k_test.pickle"
```

```
>>> dummy_list = [x*2 for x in range(10)]
>>> dummy_list # confirm what it looks like
[0, 2, 4, 6, 8, 10, 12, 14, 16, 18]
>>> with open(FILENAME,'w') as file_object: #now dump it!
        pickle.dump(dummy_list,file_object)

>>> # open the raw file to look at what was written
>>> with open(FILENAME,'r') as file_object:  # change w to r!!!
        print(file_object.read())

(lp0
I0
aI2
aI4
aI6
aI8
aI10
aI12
aI14
aI16
aI18
a.
```

You created a list object, called dummy_list, and then pickled it into the file p4k_test.pickle. You opened the file and read back its contents. It was mostly junk, but you can see an echo of the original list hidden in there.

The pickle module is to "Create portable serialized representations of Python objects" (from the docstring). Which is easy to say (try it), but rather harder to explain. Python stores its objects in your computer's memory. The way it stores it is determined, in part, by the computer you're running and the operating system that you are using. In order to transfer an object from one place (or one time) to another, it needs to be represented in a way which is independent of (apart from) those things.

Generally speaking, that's called the process of *serialization,* preparing data so it can be saved or sent. Python's `pickle` module allows you to save Python objects in a file in a way that any other Python program reading that file is able to re-create a copy of the object.

Python can't pickle just anything. It can pickle only if the object is *hashable*. It's hashable if it has __hash__ () and either the __eq__ () or __cmp__ () method. When you try to pickle more complex objects, you'll run into this problem. By then you'll be able to research your own solution.

Time to prove that you can re-create the original object. Close IDLE completely. Then restart it:

```
Python 2.7.3 (default, Apr 14 2012, 08:58:41) [GCC] on linux2
Type "copyright", "credits" or "license()" for more information.
>>> import pickle
>>> FILENAME = "p4k_test.pickle"
>>> with open(FILENAME,'r') as file_object:
        dummy_copy = pickle.load(file_object)


>>> dummy_copy
[0, 2, 4, 6, 8, 10, 12, 14, 16, 18]
```

Hey, it's the same as what you pickled. It survived in the file `p4k_test.pickle` while you turned IDLE off and on again.

To save an object called `variable_name` with the `pickle` module, follow these steps:

1. Name the file where you'll store the data.

   If it's going to be the same name every time (rather than, for example, a file name chosen by the user) then store it as a constant.

2. Open that filename with the `'w'` (write) attribute and store the file object that `open` returns.

The `with` keyword takes care of a lot of this for you: `with open(FILENAME,'w') as file_object:` I suggest you use the `'w'` so that you always overwrite the save file with a new copy of the object. You can add more objects to an existing file with the append attribute (`'a'`) but I'm not going there.

3. Call `pickle.dump(file_object, variable_name)`.

To load an object with the `pickle` module:

1. Get the name of the file where the data's been stored.

2. Open that file with the `'r'` (read) attribute and store the file object that `open` returns.

   The `with` keyword takes care of a lot of this for you: `with open(FILENAME,'r') as file_object:`

3. Call pickle's `load` method and assign it to a variable: `variable_name = pickle.load(file_object)`.

You can customize the `pickle` module. Another module, `cPickle`, isn't as customizable, but is much faster than `pickle` for saving and loading.

Use `cPickle` in your programs in the future. It's customary to refer to the module `pickle` in your code even when you're using the `cPickle` module. What? Import the `cPickle` module with an alias — `import cPickle as pickle` means everywhere else in the code. Python sees `pickle` as a reference to `cPickle`. For example, if you did `import random as crazy`, then you could call the `crazy.randint` method.

Pickle's awesome pickle power is a security risk. If someone tricks you into running `pickle.load()` on a pickle they made, they can run code on your machine. Don't unpickle any pickle unless you trust that it's yours and nobody's messed with it. When you move your skills up to The Next Level, this includes not accepting data in pickle files across a network.

Add a save Function

You can add a save function to the file fairly easily, although testing it is a little difficult. You just dump the instances to the file.

When you work on a more complicated program, include code that lets the user choose the name of the file in which to save the address book.

For this project, the filename is hard coded:

1. Add an Imports section and a Constants section.

2. Type the words import cPickle as pickle.

3. Type this in the Constants section:

   ```
   SAVE_FILE_NAME = "address_book.pickle"
   ```

4. In the AddressBook class, add a method called save.

5. In the save method, add this:

   ```
   with open(SAVE_FILE_NAME,'w') as file_object:
       pickle.dump(self, file_object)
   ```

6. In the Testing section, type address_book.save().

The new Imports and Constants sections look like this:

```
#### Imports
import cPickle as pickle

#### Constants
SAVE_FILE_NAME = "address_book.pickle"
```

This is the save method you added to the AddressBook class:

```
def save(self):
    with open(SAVE_FILE_NAME, 'w') as file_object:
        pickle.dump(self, file_object)
```

You added this line to the `Main` section:

```
address_book.save()
```

Loading a Saved Pickle in the Same Application

When you wrote the code to save the `AddressBook` instance, you made it a method of the class. It literally saved itself, and that's a problem. An object can't load itself because it won't exist until *after* it's been loaded. (Riddle me that one, PythonCoder.) The problem then is where to put the code for loading the object.

I propose that you make another class to control how the program flows are going to work and manage communications between the user and the `AddressBook` instance. That will allow you to step outside the `AddressBook` and reference it more naturally.

Create a `Controller` class

Create a `Controller` class with these steps:

1. Create a new class definition called `Controller`:

   ```
   class Controller(object):
   ```

2. Create a docstring for it. Freestyle it!

3. Give it a constructor method: `def __init__(self):`

4. In that method, create an instance of `AddressBook` as an attribute of `Controller`. Call it `address_book. self.address_book = AddressBook()`.

5. Transfer the other initialization code to this constructor method: `person1 = AddressEntry("Eric", "Idle", "March 29, 1943")`.

6. Add a `load` method to the class.

   The `load` method you create should use the formula to load an object from the `save` file, and should replace the `address_book` attribute of the `Controller`. The `load` method relies on you having already pickled an `AddressBook` instance into that file. (Save a pickle there from the command line if you need to.)

   ```
   def load(self):
       """
       Load a pickled address book from the standard save file
       """
       with open(SAVE_FILE_NAME, 'r') as file_object:
           self.address_book = pickle.load(file_object)
   ```

7. In the `Main` section, create an instance of the `Controller` class: `controller = Controller()`.

   I'm calling it a `Controller` because it's controlling the data saved in the address book. The revised code in all its glory:

   ```
   """
   Addressbook.py
   An address book program to store details of people I know.
   Stuff I'm storing is:
   first name
   family name
   email address
   date of birth
   [other stuff]

   Brendan Scott
   Feb 2015

   """
   ```

```
#### Imports
import cPickle as pickle

#### Constants
SAVE_FILE_NAME = "address_book.pickle"

##### Classes Section
class AddressBook(object):
    """
    AddressBook instances hold and manage a list of people
    """
    def __init__(self):
        """ Set people attribute to an empty list"""
        self.people = []

    def add_entry(self, new_entry):
        """ Add a new entry to the list of people in the
        address book the new_entry should be an instance
        of the AddressEntry class"""
        self.people.append(new_entry)

    def save(self):
        """ save a copy of self into a pickle file"""
        with open(SAVE_FILE_NAME, 'w') as file_object:
            pickle.dump(self, file_object)

class AddressEntry(object):
    """
    AddressEntry instances hold and manage details of a person
    """
    def __init__(self, first_name=None, family_name=None,
                 email_address=None, date_of_birth=None):
        """Initialize attributes first_name,
        family_name and date_of_birth.
        Each argument should be a string.
        date_of_birth should be of the form "MM DD, YYYY"
        """
```

```python
        self.first_name = first_name
        self.family_name = family_name
        self.email_address = email_address
        self.date_of_birth = date_of_birth

    def __repr__(self):
        """
        Given an AddressEntry object self return
        a readable string representation
        """
        template = "AddressEntry(first_name='%s', "+\
                   "family_name='%s',"+\
                   " email_address='%s', "+\
                   "date_of_birth='%s')"
        return template%(self.first_name, self.family_name,
                         self.email_address, self.date_of_birth)

class Controller(object):
    """
    Controller acts as a way of managing the data stored in
    an instance of AddressBook and the user, as well as managing
    loading of stored data
    """

    def __init__(self):
        """
        Initialise controller. Look for a saved address book
        If one is found,load it, otherwise create an empty
        address book.
        """
        self.address_book = AddressBook()
        person1 = AddressEntry("Eric", "Idle", "March 29, 1943")
        self.address_book.add_entry(person1)

    def load(self):
        """
        Load a pickled address book from the standard save file
        """
```

```
        with open(SAVE_FILE_NAME, 'r') as file_object:
            self.address_book = pickle.load(file_object)


##### Functions Section


##### Main Section


if __name__ == "__main__":
    controller = Controller()
    print(controller.address_book.people)
```

The main thing to pay attention to in this code is that I have
changed the references from address_book to self.address_
book. It makes it an attribute of the Controller instance. I also
changed the last print function from address_book.people to
controller.address_book.people. It shows that people is
an attribute of address_book and that address_book is an
attribute of controller.

This is two levels of attribute (attribute of attribute of object).
You can do as many as you like, but don't get too carried away.
It'll get hard to follow.

When you run the code, you get this:

```
[AddressEntry(first_name='Eric', family_name='Idle', email_address='March 29, 1943',
        date_of_birth='None')]
```

How does that testing help? It makes sure all the references from
the new Controller class are working. Remember that the load
method is not being tested here, since control never passes to it.

Test the load Method

To test the load method, you need an object already pickled into
the file address_book.pickle. In the final version of your application, you want the load file to run automatically when you start

it. To do that, the file should first test whether there's a save file to load. If it's there, it should load (and, if not, do nothing).

To test whether a file exists, use the `exists` method from the `os.path` module. If you pass `os.path.exists` a file path, it tells you whether a file exists at that path. Test to see if you have already saved a file. You should have saved this when running the earlier code.

```
>>> import os.path
>>> SAVE_FILE_NAME = "address_book.pickle"
>>> os.path.exists(SAVE_FILE_NAME)
True
>>> os.path.exists("some other filename that doesn't exist")
False
```

If `os.path.exists(SAVE_FILE_NAME)` is `False`, you're in trouble! Check that you've typed `SAVE_FILE_NAME = "address_book.pickle"` correctly here and in the `Constants` section of the preceding code. If it's typed correctly, then run this code in the IDLE Shell window to save a new copy:

```
>>> from address_book import SAVE_FILE_NAME
>>> from address_book import AddressBook, AddressEntry
>>> person1 = AddressEntry("Eric", "Idle", None, "March 29, 1943")
>>> address_book = AddressBook()
>>> address_book.add_entry(person1)
>>> address_book.save()
>>> import os.path # confirm it's there
>>> os.path.exists(SAVE_FILE_NAME)
True
```

Now you're going to upgrade the `Controller` so that when it's created, it checks whether there's a `save` file to load (and if there is, it loads that `save` file):

1. In your `Imports` section: `import os.path`.

2. Make the first line of the `Controller` constructor `self.address_book = self.load()`.

You're going to change the `load` method so that if there's a save file to load, then it loads `address_book` from the file and returns it. Otherwise it returns `None`.

3. Add a line to check `if self.address_book is None:`. If it is, create a new `address_book`: `self.address_book = AddressBook()`.

4. In the `load` method, test to see if `os.path.exists(SAVE_FILE_NAME)`.

5. If the file exists, change the existing code to load an object using `pickle`, then return the object loaded.

   Otherwise, return `None`.

Now the `Imports` section looks like this:

```
#### Imports
import cPickle as pickle
import os.path
```

And the `Controller` section looks like this:

```
class Controller(object):
    """
    Controller acts as a way of managing the data stored in
    an instance of AddressBook and the user, as well as managing
    loading of stored data
    """

    def __init__(self):
        """
        Initialize controller. Look for a saved address book
        If one is found, load it, otherwise create an empty
        address book.
        """
```

```python
        self.address_book = self.load()
        if self.address_book is None:
            self.address_book = AddressBook()

    def load(self):
        """
        Load a pickled address book from the standard save file
        """
        #TODO: Test this method
        if os.path.exists(SAVE_FILE_NAME):
            with open(SAVE_FILE_NAME, 'r') as file_object:
                return pickle.load(file_object)
        else:
            return None
```

I tested this both when the file was there and when it wasn't. You should too. Be careful!

Add an Interface

The final thing you need to do for this project is add an interface to add, delete, and show address book entries:

1. Give the user some instructions and a prompt to confirm a quit. Add this in the `Constants` section:

```python
INSTRUCTIONS = """Address Book Application
(Python For Kids For Dummies Project 9)
Press:
a to add an entry
d to display a list of all entries in summary form.
i to print these instructions again
q to quit.
"""
CONFIRM_QUIT_MESSAGE = 'Are you sure you want to quit (Y/n)? '
```

2. Read those instructions yourself, because that's what you're going to be coding to.

3. Add a new method called `run_interface` in `Controller`: `def run_interface(self):`.

   Don't forget your `self`!

4. Add `self.run_interface()` at the end of the `Controller` constructor.

5. In `run_interface`, show the instructions `print (INSTRUCTIONS)`. Then create an infinite `while` loop: `while True:`.

   The `while` loop is the program's context. In each iteration it should:

   - Ask the user what they want to do: `command = raw_input("What would you like to do? ")`. Then see what the user's command is.

   - Respond to the user's command. Use an `if/elif` clause to check for each option listed in the `INSTRUCTIONS` constant.

   - Create a method stub (in `Controller`) for `add_entry` and `display_summaries`. Add a call to that stub at the corresponding point in the `if` clause. For example, the code to deal with `"a"` (for add entry) is

   ```
   if command == "a":
       self.add_entry()
   ```

   - If the user chooses to quit `elif command == "q":` then call `confirm_quit`. Copy and paste the code for the `confirm_quit` function across from Project 5 (`guess_game_fun.py`) into the `Functions` section. If the quit is confirmed, print a message saying that the application is saving `print("Saving")`, call `address_book`'s save method, then `break` (out of the loop), and let the program end.

- If the user has not typed a command listed in the instructions, say so. At the end of the `if` block include an `else:` which tells the user you don't understand their instructions `print("I don't recognise that instruction (%s)"%command)`

6. Create a method stub for `add_entry` and `display_summaries`.

   Each stub should include a docstring explaining the method and a `print` statement so you can make sure the correct function is being called for each possible command given. An example for `add_entry`:

   ```
   def add_entry(self):
       """query user for values to add a new entry"""
       print("In add_entry")
   ```

The `AddressBook` and `AddressEntry` classes are unchanged, as are the `Imports` and `Main` sections. The new `Constants` section looks like this:

```
#### Constants
SAVE_FILE_NAME = "address_book.pickle"
INSTRUCTIONS = """Address Book Application
(Python For Kids For Dummies Project 9)
Press:
a to add an entry
d to display a list of all entries in summary form.
i to print these instructions again
q to quit.
"""
CONFIRM_QUIT_MESSAGE = 'Are you sure you want to quit (Y/n)? '
```

In `Controller`, the constructor looks like this. Only the last line is new:

```
def __init__(self):
    """
    Initialize controller. Look for a saved address book
    If one is found,load it, otherwise create an empty
```

```
address book.
"""
self.address_book = self.load()
if self.address_book is None:
    self.address_book = AddressBook()

self.run_interface()
```

I also added interface related methods to `Controller` (after the end of the `load` method) and copied across `confirm_quit` from Project 5 into the `Functions` section:

```
def run_interface(self):
    """ Application's main loop.
    Get user input and respond accordingly"""

    print(INSTRUCTIONS)
    while True:
        command = raw_input("What would you like to do? ")
        if command == "a":
            self.add_entry()
        elif command == "q":
            if confirm_quit():
                print("Saving")
                self.address_book.save()
                print("Exiting the application")
                break
        elif command == "i":
            print(INSTRUCTIONS)
        elif command == "d":
            self.display_summaries()
        else:
            template = "I don't recognise that instruction (%s)"
            print(template%command)

def add_entry(self):
    """query user for values to add a new entry"""
    print("In add_entry")
```

```
def display_summaries(self):
    """ display summary information for each entry in
    address book"""
    print("In display_summaries")

##### Functions Section
def confirm_quit():
    """Ask user to confirm that they want to quit
    default to yes
    Return True (yes, quit) or False (no, don't quit) """
    spam = raw_input(CONFIRM_QUIT_MESSAGE)
    if spam == 'n':
        return False
    else:
        return True
```

I ran the code and tested that each command called the correct method. You need to test your code as well to make sure that for these commands, it prints certain things:

✔ a = "In add_entry"

✔ d = "In display_summaries"

✔ i = instructions again

✔ q = quit confirmation

✔ You also need to check if you type something else (eg r) it prints "I don't recognize that instruction (r)".

✔ Note that you now have two add_entry methods. The first is in the AddressBook class, the second is in the Controller class. They can live in harmony because the name of the class allows you to distinguish between the two of them. In fact, the add_entry method in the Controller class will even call the add_entry method in the AddressBook class.

Fill in the Methods

To finish off the application, add code that makes the methods `add_entry` and `display_summaries` work.

The method `add_entry` is supposed to add an address book entry. To do that you need to get values for `first_name`, `last_name`, `email_address`, and `date_of_birth`.

1. Give the user some information:

   ```
   print("Adding a new person to the address book")
   print("What is the person's:")
   ```

2. Use a `raw_input` statement to get a value for each of the attributes.

   This is an example for `first_name`:

   ```
   first_name = raw_input("First Name? ")
   ```

3. For each of these, add a test to see if the user typed q.

   If so, don't add the entry (just `return`). The code for `first_name` (repeat this code, but change the name of the variable for the other attributes) would be this:

   ```
   if first_name == "q":
       print("Not Adding")
       return
   ```

4. Use the values you collect to create an `AddressEntry` and add it to `AddressBook`. The code `entry = AddressEntry (first_name, family_name, date_of_birth)` is a single line of code.

   ```
   entry = AddressEntry(first_name, family_name,
           date_of_birth)
   self.address_book.add_entry(entry)
   ```

   For `display_summaries`, use `enumerate` to list all the people in `AddressBook`.

Each will be an `AddressEntry` instance. Make a template (in the `Constants` section) like:

```
SUMMARY_TEMPLATE = "%s %s DOB: %s email: %s"
```

In the `for` loop, use this template to format each of the attributes `first_name`, `last_name`, `date_of_birth`, and `email_address` into a dummy variable. Then print the index (add one) and the entry using a short formatting string like `"%s: %s"`. This will print a summary of each entry with numbering. Some sample code:

```
for index, e in enumerate(self.address_book.people):
    values = (e.first_name, e.family_name,
              e.date_of_birth, e.email_address)
    entry = SUMMARY_TEMPLATE%values
    print("%s: %s"%(index+1, entry))
    # start numbering at 1
```

6. Remove the code `print(controller.address_book.people)` at the end of the `Main` section

You don't need it for debugging anymore. Now the code in `Main` section is very simple. It's mainly just `controller = Controller()`. The program flow is a little different in this example. After `controller` is instantiated, control passes to its constructor and, from there, to its `run_interface` method. It only leaves the `run_interface` method when it's time to quit. You'll see this structure more often as you work with Python.

The Complete Code

Your final version of the code should look something like this:

```
"""
Addressbook.py
An address book program to store details of people I know.
Stuff I'm storing is:
first name
```

```
        family name
        email address
        date of birth
        [other stuff]


        Brendan Scott
        Feb 2015


        """


        #### Imports
        import cPickle as pickle
        import os.path


        #### Constants
        SAVE_FILE_NAME = "address_book.pickle"
        INSTRUCTIONS = """Address Book Application
        (Python For Kids For Dummies Project 9)
        Press:
        a to add an entry
        d to display a list of all entries in summary form.
        i to print these instructions again
        q to quit.
        """
        CONFIRM_QUIT_MESSAGE = 'Are you sure you want to quit (Y/n)? '
        SUMMARY_TEMPLATE = "%s %s DOB: %s email: %s"


        ##### Classes Section
        class AddressBook(object):
            """

            AddressBook instances hold and manage a list of people
            """

            def __init__(self):
                """ Set people attribute to an empty list"""
                self.people = []


            def add_entry(self, new_entry):
                """ Add a new entry to the list of people in the
                address book the new_entry should be an instance
```

```
        of the AddressEntry class"""
        self.people.append(new_entry)

    def save(self):
        """ save a copy of self into a pickle file"""
        with open(SAVE_FILE_NAME, 'w') as file_object:
            pickle.dump(self, file_object)


class AddressEntry(object):
    """
    AddressEntry instances hold and manage details of a person
    """
    def __init__(self, first_name=None, family_name=None,
                 email_address=None, date_of_birth=None):
        """"Initialize attributes first_name,
        family_name and date_of_birth.
        Each argument should be a string.
        date_of_birth should be of the form "MM DD, YYYY"
        """
        self.first_name = first_name
        self.family_name = family_name
        self.email_address = email_address
        self.date_of_birth = date_of_birth

    def __repr__(self):
        """
        Given an AddressEntry object self return
        a readable string representation
        """
        template = "AddressEntry(first_name='%s', "+\
                   "family_name='%s',"+\
                   " email_address='%s', "+\
                   "date_of_birth='%s')"
        return template%(self.first_name, self.family_name,
                         self.email_address, self.date_of_birth)
```

```python
class Controller(object):
    """
    Controller acts as a way of managing the data stored in
    an instance of AddressBook and the user, as well as managing
    loading of stored data
    """

    def __init__(self):
        """
        Initialize controller. Look for a saved address book
        If one is found,load it, otherwise create an empty
        address book.
        """
        self.address_book = self.load()
        if self.address_book is None:
            self.address_book = AddressBook()

        self.run_interface()

    def load(self):
        """
        Load a pickled address book from the standard save file
        """
        if os.path.exists(SAVE_FILE_NAME):
            with open(SAVE_FILE_NAME, 'r') as file_object:
                address_book = pickle.load(file_object)
            return address_book
        else:
            return None

    def run_interface(self):
        """ Application's main loop.
        Get user input and respond accordingly"""

        print(INSTRUCTIONS)
        while True:
            command = raw_input("What would you like to do? ")
```

```python
            if command == "a":
                self.add_entry()
            elif command == "q":
                if confirm_quit():
                    print("Saving")
                    self.address_book.save()
                    print("Exiting the application")
                    break
            elif command == "i":
                print(INSTRUCTIONS)
            elif command == "d":
                self.display_summaries()
            else:
                template = "I don't recognise that instruction (%s)"
                print(template%command)


    def add_entry(self):
        """query user for values to add a new entry"""
        print("Adding a new person to the address book")
        print("What is the person's:")
        first_name = raw_input("First Name? ")
        if first_name == "q":
            print("Not Adding")
            return
        family_name = raw_input("Family Name? ")
        if family_name == "q":
            print("Not Adding")
            return
        email_address = raw_input("Email Address? ")
        if email_address == "q":
            print("Not Adding")
            return
        DOB_PROMPT = "Date of Birth (Month day, year)? "
        date_of_birth = raw_input(DOB_PROMPT)
        if date_of_birth == "q":
            print("Not Adding ")
            return
```

```
            entry = AddressEntry(first_name, family_name,
                             email_address, date_of_birth)
            self.address_book.add_entry(entry)
            values = (first_name, family_name)
            print("Added address entry for %s %s\n"%values)

    def display_summaries(self):
        """ display summary information for each entry in
        address book"""
        print("Displaying Summaries")
        for index, e in enumerate(self.address_book.people):
            values = (e.first_name, e.family_name,
                      e.date_of_birth, e.email_address)
            entry = SUMMARY_TEMPLATE%values
            print("%s: %s"%(index+1, entry))
            # start numbering at 1

##### Functions Section
def confirm_quit():
    """Ask user to confirm that they want to quit
    default to yes
    Return True (yes, quit) or False (no, don't quit) """
    spam = raw_input(CONFIRM_QUIT_MESSAGE)
    if spam == 'n':
        return False
    else:
        return True

##### Main Section

if __name__ == "__main__":
    controller = Controller()
```

Summary

You made it through a big fat project! This code gives you a solid
core for an address book application that you can expand — for
example, use the Cryptopy project to add secret notes, change the

`AddressBook` so that when you add an entry it sorts the list in alphabetical order, add new fields (special skills?), calculate the person's age from their date of birth (research the `datetime` module), and when you do the Hello GUI World project, wrap a graphical interface around the app. The possibilities are endless.

You're introduced to tons in this project:

- Defining your own custom objects with classes.

- Creating objects from your definitions with instances.

- That classes, like all objects, can have attributes.

- The difference between class attributes and instance attributes.

- How instances can inherit the attributes of their defining class, but not vice versa.

- What a constructor method (`__init__`) is and how it runs each time you create an instance.

- Passing parameters to `__init__` to prefill instances with data.

- What overriding is, and how overriding `__repr__` lets you get a different printout for your object.

- Adding methods to your classes.

- How `self` is automatically passed as an argument when you call your class methods.

- Saving and loading general Python objects with the power of `pickle`.

- Using the `os.path` module to see if a file exists on your file system.

- Reusing and applying some earlier concepts: `if/elif/else` blocks, opening files, `enumerate`, `raw_input`, and formatting strings.

Math Trainer

Do *you* want a chance to be the teacher? This project tests users on their times tables and displays times tables so a user can practice. It keeps score and records how long it took to take the test.

Here's where you put your class skills to the test and give your brain a workout.

```
*Python 2.7.9 Shell*
File  Edit  Shell  Debug  Options  Windows  Help
>>> ============================= RESTART =============================
>>>
Welcome to Math Trainer
This application will train you on your times tables.
It can either print one or more of the tables for you
so that you can revise (training) or you it can test
you on your times tables.

Press 1 for training.  Press 2 for testing. Press 3 to quit.
1

In this section you can print out tables that you need to revise.
Type in a list of the multiplication tables that you want to revise,
separated by commas. You can specify a range of tables.  For example,
4-6 means tables 4, 5 and 6.
If you have finished revising, enter q.
What tables would you like to revise?
5,7,9-11
   5 x   1 =    5   7 x   1 =    7   9 x   1 =    9  10 x   1 =   10  11 x   1 =   11
   5 x   2 =   10   7 x   2 =   14   9 x   2 =   18  10 x   2 =   20  11 x   2 =   22
   5 x   3 =   15   7 x   3 =   21   9 x   3 =   27  10 x   3 =   30  11 x   3 =   33
   5 x   4 =   20   7 x   4 =   28   9 x   4 =   36  10 x   4 =   40  11 x   4 =   44
   5 x   5 =   25   7 x   5 =   35   9 x   5 =   45  10 x   5 =   50  11 x   5 =   55
   5 x   6 =   30   7 x   6 =   42   9 x   6 =   54  10 x   6 =   60  11 x   6 =   66
   5 x   7 =   35   7 x   7 =   49   9 x   7 =   63  10 x   7 =   70  11 x   7 =   77
   5 x   8 =   40   7 x   8 =   56   9 x   8 =   72  10 x   8 =   80  11 x   8 =   88
   5 x   9 =   45   7 x   9 =   63   9 x   9 =   81  10 x   9 =   90  11 x   9 =   99
   5 x  10 =   50   7 x  10 =   70   9 x  10 =   90  10 x  10 =  100  11 x  10 =  110
   5 x  11 =   55   7 x  11 =   77   9 x  11 =   99  10 x  11 =  110  11 x  11 =  121
   5 x  12 =   60   7 x  12 =   84   9 x  12 =  108  10 x  12 =  120  11 x  12 =  132


Welcome to Math Trainer
This application will train you on your times tables.
It can either print one or more of the tables for you
so that you can revise (training) or you it can test
you on your times tables.

Press 1 for training.  Press 2 for testing. Press 3 to quit.
                                                          Ln: 30 Col: 69
```

Planning Your Math Trainer

Your math trainer should ask for answers about the times tables (from 1 through 12) and make sure the answer is right.

But does your best friend need help memorizing the tables? The math trainer could print out a times table. Maybe your other BFF knows the smaller numbers already, so the trainer should set a bottom limit (just avoid the 1s, for instance). If you like, you can add a higher upper limit than 12.

Add a score and time how long it takes to take the test. Game on!

Setting Up

Set up your file and put some code in that asks a question and works out whether the answer is correct.

Do the following to get the project up and running:

1. Create a new file called `math_trainer.py`.

2. Create a module docstring for the file.

3. Use a hash comment to mark these sections: `Imports`, `Constants`, `Function`, and `Testing`.

   You know from the silly sentences project that if you put a tuple after a formatting operator `%`, Python unpacks the tuple into formatting specifiers in the formatting string. That means that `"What is %sx%s?"%(4,6)` becomes `"What is 4x6?"`. You're going to store each question as a tuple with two numbers.

4. Make a question to use for testing. Create a `TEST_QUESTION` constant in the `Constants` section. Choose two numbers as a test and set `TEST_QUESTION` equal to the tuple containing them.

This example is `(4,6)`. You can use it or think up some other numbers.

5. Create a constant called `QUESTION_TEMPLATE`.

   It'll be a formatting template for your test question. Set it to `"What is %sx%s"` (or another template if you can think of one).

6. Create a new variable `question` and make it equal to `TEST_QUESTION`.

   Use that new variable in your code. Later you'll list questions and get them one by one from the list. You'll change the value of `question`, and the rest of the program will work with the new questions — without any other changes.

7. In the `Testing` section, create a prompt to use in a `raw_input` command by feeding the tuple `question` into the formatting string `QUESTION_TEMPLATE`.

8. Add a line that calculates the correct answer (by multiplying `question[0]` and `question[1]` together).

9. Use the prompt you created in a `raw_input` statement to get the user's answer.

10. Change the user's answer to a number (use `int`).

11. Check the user's answer against the correct answer and print `Correct!` or `Incorrect`.

Here's my code:

```
"""
math_trainer.py
Train your times tables.
Initial Features:
* Print out times table for a given number.
```

```
* Limit tables to a lower number (default is 1)
and an upper number (default is 12).
* Pose test questions to the user
* Check whether the user is right or wrong
* Track the user's score.
Brendan Scott
February 2015
"""


#### Constants Section
TEST_QUESTION = (4, 6)
QUESTION_TEMPLATE = "What is %sx%s? "


#### Function Section

#### Testing Section

question = TEST_QUESTION
prompt = QUESTION_TEMPLATE%question
correct_answer = question[0]*question[1] # indexes start from 0
answer = raw_input(prompt)
if int(answer)== correct_answer:
    print("Correct!")
else:
    print("Incorrect")
```

Run to test it:

```
>>> ================================ RESTART
================================
>>>
What is 4x6? 24
Correct!
>>> ================================ RESTART
================================
>>>
What is 4x6? 25
Incorrect
```

Test twice — once for when the answer is right and once for when the answer is wrong.

Create Questions

You could create the questions in this trainer using the `random.randint` function or even `random.choice` to create the questions. The problem is that you can't make sure that the whole times table is tested. Your random number might never give you an 8, for example.

Instead, generate the whole list of possible questions (12x12 = 144 of them) and pick questions from that list. That way you can keep track of what you've picked and throw out some other questions. Way back in Project 2 I told you that using the `range` built-in in Python 2.7 can use up memory. This many entries is manageable, so using `range` here is okay.

To create your question list, follow along:

1. In the `Function` section, define a function called `make_question_list`.

2. Write a short docstring for the function.

3. Specify the upper and lower limits of each number in the questions.

   To do that, add `lower` and `upper` as arguments to your function. Add default values to the arguments in the function: `lower = 1` and `upper = 12`:

   ```
   def make_question_list(lower=LOWER, upper=UPPER):
   ```

   This structure — `lower=LOWER` — looks odd, but it makes sense. LOWER is a constant with a default value, and `lower` is the name of the variable that will be used within the function.

4. Use a double list comprehension to create a list of tuples:

```
return [(x+1, y+1) for x in range(lower-1, upper)
                   for y in range(lower-1, upper)]
```

5. Return the list as the function's return value.

6. Comment out the existing `Testing` section.

   Don't delete it; you'll need it again later.

7. Add a line in the `Testing` section to call the function and print the value that it gets back.

I added constants to the `Constants` section to avoid *magic numbers* (numbers that appear magically without any explanation in your code):

```
#### Constants
TEST_QUESTION = (4, 6)
QUESTION_TEMPLATE = "What is %sx%s? "
LOWER = 1
UPPER = 12
```

The `Function` section has a new function in it:

```
#### Function Section
def make_question_list(lower=LOWER, upper=UPPER):
    """ prepare a list of questions in the form (x,y)
    where x and y are in the range from LOWER to UPPER inclusive
    """

    return [(x+1, y+1) for x in range(lower-1, upper)
                       for y in range(lower-1, upper)]
```

This function really only has one line of code — the double list comprehension. The list comprehension was tough because `range(lower, upper)` goes up to, but doesn't include `upper`. That's not what was specified in the statement of requirements. To account for this the generated tuples add 1 to both the numbers (x+1, y+1). It's also the reason that lower value has -1 in both list comprehensions.

Minus (math pun) the code commented out, the Testing section now looks like this:

```
#### Testing Section

question_list = make_question_list()
print(question_list)
```

When you run it, you get a list of 144 tuples ranging from (1,1), (1,2) . . .(12,11), (12,12). That's good.

This test shows that the function works for the default values. Test it with a couple other values just in case. Change the Testing section to this:

1. Choose two or three values to pass as lower and two or three values to pass as upper. Make them pairs of lower and upper.

2. Call make_question_list. Pass the lower and upper value pairs.

3. Print the results each time.

This is the new Testing section:

```
#### Testing Section

for lower,upper in [(2, 5), (4, 6), (7, 11)]:
    question_list = make_question_list(lower, upper)
    print(question_list)
```

Can you see what's happening? The for loop runs through a list with three elements in it. Each element is a two-tuple. Each element is unpacked into the variables lower and upper, in order. For each of those values, the function is called and the question list it creates is printed.

This is what I got:

```
[(2, 2), (2, 3), (2, 4), (2, 5), (3, 2), (3, 3), (3, 4), (3, 5),
         (4, 2), (4, 3), (4, 4), (4, 5), (5, 2), (5, 3),
         (5, 4), (5, 5)]
 [(4, 4), (4, 5), (4, 6), (5, 4), (5, 5), (5, 6), (6, 4),
         (6, 5), (6, 6)]
 [(7, 7), (7, 8), (7, 9), (7, 10), (7, 11), (8, 7), (8, 8), (8, 9),
         (8, 10), (8, 11), (9, 7), (9, 8), (9, 9), (9, 10),
         (9, 11), (10, 7), (10, 8), (10, 9), (10, 10), (10, 11),
         (11, 7), (11, 8), (11, 9), (11, 10), (11, 11)]
```

Ask Lots of Questions in a Row

You have a list of questions and you know how to ask any one of them. The next step is to bombard your user with questions — boom, boom, boom. If you try to step through the questions one at a time, you run into two problems:

✔ The list is in times table order, so it's not much of a test. It's better to make it random.

✔ The list has 144 items. Unless you're really, really mean, you probably don't want to force the user to do all of them at one time. It's better to ask a certain number of questions at one time.

No worries! You can solve these problems.

Put questions in a random order

You can sort the table into random order:

1. At the top of the file, add an `Imports` section and `import` the `random` module.

2. Add an optional argument `random_order` to the function `make_question_list`.

The argument should have a default value of `True` (or `False`, if you prefer your questions to be in the right order).

3. Update the docstring to explain what the `random_order` argument is going to do.

4. Store the list of questions generated in a dummy variable.

   It's a dummy variable, so call it something short. I'm going to call it `spam`.

5. Test whether `random_order` is `True`.

   `if random_order:` is good enough, but if that makes you uncomfortable, try `if random_order is True:`

   If it is `True`, apply `random.shuffle(spam)` to the dummy variable. You shouldn't need an `else:` block. Use `help(random.shuffle)` in the IDLE Shell window to confirm what `random.shuffle` does and what its return value is (warning: trick!).

6. Return the dummy variable.

This is the new `Imports` section:

```
#### Imports Section
import random
```

The new `Function` section looks like this:

```
#### Function Section
def make_question_list(lower=LOWER, upper=UPPER, random_order=True):
    """ prepare a list of questions in the form (x,y)
    where x and y are in the range from LOWER to UPPER inclusive
    If random_order is true, rearrange the questions in a random order
    """
    spam = [(x+1, y+1) for x in range(lower-1,upper)
                       for y in range(lower-1,upper)]
    if random_order:
        random.shuffle(spam)
    return spam
```

Leave the `Testing` section the same. It's easier to review the shorter lists.

This is what you get when you run it:

```
[(4, 2), (3, 4), (4, 4), (5, 2), (5, 4), (2, 5), (3, 2), (2, 4),
        (3, 5), (5, 3), (2, 3), (4, 3), (5, 5), (2, 2),
        (4, 5), (3, 3)]
[(5, 6), (4, 5), (6, 5), (5, 4), (6, 4), (5, 5), (4, 4), (4, 6),
        (6, 6)]
[(11, 7), (8, 11), (9, 8), (11, 10), (9, 7), (7, 7), (10, 8),
        (9, 10), (8, 10), (10, 10), (9, 11), (7, 10), (10, 7),
        (7, 11), (8, 9), (11, 8), (11, 11), (8, 7), (10, 11),
        (9, 9), (7, 8), (10, 9), (11, 9), (7, 9), (8, 8)]
```

Your shuffled list will look different because it's, yanno, random. Compare these to the unshuffled versions. Just as an example, the first unshuffled list ought to start with (2,2).

You've added a new variable, `random_order`, which can be `True` or `False`. It defaults to `True`, so you've only tested one option so far. You should also test what happens when `random_order` is `False`. (The function should return unshuffled lists like before you added the variable.) To do that, change the code so it passes `False` into the function (`question_list = make_question_list(lower, upper, False)`) and check that it returns an unshuffled list.

Ask a certain number of questions at a time

It's pretty easy to pose multiple questions — put them in a loop. When you ask multiple questions, though, the next logical thing to do is to keep track of the score.

To ask multiple questions and keep track of the score:

1. Comment out the code in the `Testing` section that was used to test variations on `make_question_list`.

2. Create a constant for the total number of questions to be asked (MAX_QUESTIONS = 3). Add it to the Constants section.

   Use a small number so you don't have too many numbers to test against. I chose 3.

3. In the Functions section, create a function called do_testing. (It doesn't need to take arguments.)

4. In that function, create a variable to hold the user's score. Initialize to 0.

   Initializing is when you assign a value to a variable for the first time.

5. Still in the function, add a line creating a question_list by calling make_question_list().

6. In that function, create an enumerate loop that runs through the questions in question_list.

   ```
   for i, question in enumerate(question_list):
   ```

7. For each iteration of the loop, enumerate(question_list) returns a number (i in this case) and a question (a two-tuple) from the list.

   The number i is how far through the list you are (starting at 0).

   Each iteration tests to see if i is larger than or equal to the MAX_QUESTIONS constant. If it is, you've asked enough questions so use break to get out of the loop.

8. Go back to the code in the Testing section that you commented out in Step 6 of the "Create Questions" section earlier in this project.

   Uncomment it, apart from the line question=TEST_QUESTION — you don't need that. Move it to the end of the do_testing function and then indent it one level to make it part of the for loop's code block.

9. In the code block that tells users they are correct, increase the score by 1.

10. Print the user's score after the end of the questions.

11. In the `Testing` section, add a call to the new function `do_testing`.

The new `Constants` section looks like this:

```
#### Constants Section
TEST_QUESTION = (4, 6)
QUESTION_TEMPLATE = "What is %sx%s? "
LOWER = 1
UPPER = 12
MAX_QUESTIONS = 3 # for testing, you can increase it later
```

The new `do_testing` function is mostly recycled code:

```
def do_testing():
    """ conduct a round of testing """
    question_list = make_question_list()
    score = 0
    for i, question in enumerate(question_list):
        if i >= MAX_QUESTIONS:
            break
        prompt = QUESTION_TEMPLATE%question
        correct_answer = question[0]*question[1]
        # indexes start from 0
        answer = raw_input(prompt)

        if int(answer) == correct_answer:
            print("Correct!")
            score = score+1
        else:
            print("Incorrect, should have been %s"%(correct_answer))

    print("You scored %s"%score)
```

You use `enumerate` in `do_testing`, rather than `for i in range(MAX_QUESTIONS) :`. If `MAX_QUESTIONS` is too big, it could be longer than the number of questions in the list, causing an error.

Now `enumerate` will stop of its own accord at the end of the list, regardless of how big `MAX_QUESTIONS` is. Added bonus: `enumerate` is the more Pythonic way to do it.

And in the new `Testing` section, I deleted everything that wasn't reused:

```
#### Testing Section


do_testing()
```

Running this code gives you this:

```
What is 7x6? 42
Correct!
What is 11x12? 132
Correct!
What is 6x7? 24
Incorrect, should have been 42
You scored 2
```

Everything is working as it should be.

Print Out a Times Table

Printing out a times table for a given number isn't too hard. Given a value like `(4,6)`, you already know how to calculate the answer and print it in a formatted way. You shouldn't have any trouble putting together a format string to print each entry of the times table.

What *is* a little tricky is how you want it to look. Should it be one column with each problem on a separate line? That wastes a lot of screen space. Should you have multiple columns? You don't know how wide the screen is, and how many columns you can use, until you get to the end of the line. You have to decide all these interface design questions.

Start printing out the whole times table:

1. Create a constant to be used as a template for each times table entry. The constant needs to print out three numbers as a multiplication problem.

```
TIMES_TABLE_ENTRY = "%s x %s = %s"
```

You're going to accumulate these entries and then print them all at once.

2. Create a function called `display_times_tables`, in the `Functions` section, that takes one argument `upper`.

Make `upper` default to UPPER, the constant you defined earlier. UPPER equals 12:

```
def display_times_tables(upper=UPPER):
```

The argument `upper` is the largest times in the table. Change UPPER to get larger tables if you want them, but know this — they'll get big quickly.

3. Write a docstring for the function.

4. In the function, create two `for` loops, one inside the other.

Each loop should range up to the local variable `upper`. (Note the lowercase `upper`.) Call the dummy variables `x` and `y`. They're going to be the two numbers being multiplied together.

```
for x in range(upper):
    for y in range(upper):
```

5. Inside the `for y` loop, use the template string to create a string to print out the number, the index, and the product of the two of them. Then print it.

This code will prepare the output. Then you need to print `entry`:

```
entry = TIMES_TABLE_ENTRY%(x+1, y+1, (x+1)*(y+1))
```

6. Comment out the contents of the existing `Testing` section.

7. Add a line calling `display_times_tables`.

This is the template string in the `Constants` section:

```
TIMES_TABLE_ENTRY = "%s x %s = %s"
```

Here's how the `display` function looks:

```
def display_times_tables(upper=UPPER):
    """
    Display the times tables up to UPPER
    """
    for x in range(upper):
        for y in range(upper):
            entry = TIMES_TABLE_ENTRY%(x+1, y+1, (x+1)*(y+1))
            print(entry)
```

When I first did this function, I forgot to add 1 to `y`, so the times table started at `1x0` and ended at `1x11`.

The `Testing` section looks like this:

```
#### Testing Section

#do_testing()
display_times_tables()
```

Run it to get this:

```
1 x 1 = 1
1 x 2 = 2
[140 lines omitted]
12 x 11 = 132
12 x 12 = 144
```

It's working right, but the alignment is a little wonky. Double digits throw things off; triple-digit numbers will, too.

You used the `%s` specifier in the silly sentences project, but `%i` is specifically for numbers. It lets you set a minimum width for the numbers you print. For example, `%2i` sets a minimum width of 2 and `%3i` is a minimum width of 3.

On the left, make a width of 2 (since the largest number is 12, which has two digits) and on the right side of 3 (since the largest number will be 144). This is called *left padding*.

Here's a tidy format string:

```
TIMES_TABLE_ENTRY = "%2i x %2i = %3i"
```

If you make this change and rerun the program, you get this:

```
 1 x  1 =    1
 1 x  2 =    2
[140 lines omitted]
12 x 11 = 132
12 x 12 = 144
```

Hey, that's much neater! All the numbers are lined up on the right. This code won't fail if you specify a large number (like `1000`) for the times table, but the output won't be neatly aligned.

It's possible to write code that can handle any size number and nicely line things up, but part of programming is knowing when to compromise. Most times tables run from 1 through 12, so I think this is a good compromise.

Print Multiple Tables Across the Screen

The times tables are too far down the screen. A lot of the horizontal space on the screen isn't being used. This'll be better if tables are horizontal. To do that, you need to know how wide each entry is.

The `len()` built-in gives you the length of an object like a string or a list.

In the IDLE Shell window, make a sample `entry` and get its length. Like this:

```
>>> TIMES_TABLE_ENTRY = "%2i x %2i = %3i"
>>> entry = TIMES_TABLE_ENTRY%(12,12,144)
>>> len(entry)
13
```

This means that there are 13 characters in `12 x 12 = 144`. Adding a space to separate them horizontally makes 14. Programs tend to assume that a screen is about 70 characters wide. You'll use this as your benchmark. 70 divided by 14 is 5, so you can fit five times tables across the width of the screen.

To print a more compact series of times tables, you have to replace the `display_times_tables` function with code that does the following:

1. In the `Constants` section, add a blank space at the end of the constant `TIMES_TABLE_ENTRY`:

   ```
   TIMES_TABLE_ENTRY = "%2i x %2i = %3i ".
   ```

2. Create a local variable `tables_per_line` set it to 5.

3. Make a list of all the tables to be printed:

   ```
   tables_to_print = range(1, upper+1)
   ```

4. Slice off the first `tables_per_line` from `tables_to_print` and save the remainder of the list back in `tables_to_print`.

   ```
   batch = tables_to_print[:tables_per_line]
   tables_to_print = tables_to_print[tables_per_line:]
   ```

5. Create a `while` loop that executes `while batch != []:`.

6. In that `loop:`, create a `for` loop that ranges from 1 to upper+1 (to get the numbers from 1 to upper, including upper).

```
for x in range(1, upper+1):
```

7. In this `for x` loop, create an empty list to hold one line of times tables entries: `accumulator = []`.

   You make this assignment here so that it resets each time you go through the `for x` loop.

8. Create another `for` loop. This one should be `for y in batch:`.

9. Within this `for y` loop — watch the indents — add a times table entry to the `accumulator`:

```
accumulator.append(TIMES_TABLE_ENTRY%(y, x, x*y))
```

10. At the indent level of the `for x` loop, join up the accumulator with an empty string `""` and print it: `print("".join(accumulator))`.

11. Slice off another batch and shrink `tables_to_print`.

   This is the same code from Step 4 (but indented).

The final code has one space added at the end of TIMES_TABLE_ ENTRY in the `Constants` section:

```
TIMES_TABLE_ENTRY = "%2i x %2i = %3i "
```

And a revised `display_times_tables` function:

```
def display_times_tables(upper=UPPER):
    """
    Display the times tables up to UPPER
    """
    tables_per_line = 5
    tables_to_print = range(1, upper+1)
```

```
# get a batch of 5 to print
batch = tables_to_print[:tables_per_line]
# remove them from the list
tables_to_print = tables_to_print[tables_per_line:]
while batch != []: # stop when there's no more to print
    for x in range(1, upper+1):
        # this goes from 1 to 12 and is the rows
        accumulator = []
        for y in batch:
            # this covers only the tables in the batch
            # it builds the columns
            accumulator.append(TIMES_TABLE_ENTRY%(y, x, x*y))
        print("".join(accumulator)) # print one row
    print("\n") # vertical separation between blocks of tables.
    # now get another batch and repeat.
    batch = tables_to_print[:tables_per_line]
    tables_to_print = tables_to_print[tables_per_line:]
```

The while loop splits the tables (1 through 12) into batches of
five at a time. The y loop puts together each row for any given x.
For the first row, x+1 is 1, and y goes from 1 to 5, so the first row
is 1x1, 2x1, up to 5x1. For the second row, x+1 will be 2. The y
still goes from 1 to 5, so the second row will be 2x1, 2x2, and on
up to 5x2. This goes until all tables are printed.

Start on the User Interface

So far in this project, you've been working on *back-end
functionality* — things that go on behind the user interface. While
users have a little bit of interaction, they can't control what the
program does. For example, they have no instructions and can't
choose testing over training.

Yeah, really it's truly a user interface, even though it's just text on
the command line. Think carefully about the interface so your program is usable. Fantastic functionality is no good if the interface is
too hard to use. Many apps seem to spend far more time on
graphics than they do on what's behind them.

Because you only have text to work with, your user interface will be pretty simple. That said, not having to worry about beauty helps you focus on how the program will go from the time the user runs it.

Your math trainer's user interface should:

- ✔ Introduce the program to the user and explain the options — training, testing, or quit. The explanation could say, "Hey, I'm a times table trainer that prints out the times tables and I test your multiplication chops with questions." Choose numbers that the user will type to run each option and list them in the instructions.

- ✔ Ask the user which option to run.

- ✔ Pass control to the part of the program that handles that choice.

- ✔ Allow each part of the program to return control to the main part of the program. For example, users should be able to train on one of their times tables, then, when they're finished, run the `Testing` section.

- ✔ Either pass control back to the main part of the program, or let the user run that section again.

The good news is most of this is already done! Now start on these by laying down a skeleton of the code:

1. In the `Constants` section, create a constant called `INSTRUCTIONS`. Assign to this constant some introductory text and some instructions.

   When putting together this string, imagine that it's a docstring. Use triple double quotes to start it, and let it go over multiple lines.

Don't worry if you come up blank. If you're having trouble, leave INSTRUCTIONS empty, do the other steps, and then come back to it. Maybe something like:

```
INSTRUCTIONS = """Welcome to Math Trainer
This application will train you on your times tables.
It can either print one or more of the tables for you
so that you can revise (training) or it can test
your times tables.
"""
```

2. Comment out the Testing section and add a Main section at the end of the program.

3. In the Main section, add a if __name__ == "__main__": block.

4. In that block, create a while True: loop.

5. In that block, print the instructions.

   Then use "Press 1 for training. Press 2 for testing. Press 3 to quit" as a prompt for a raw_input. Store the value you get from raw_input in a variable called selection.

   The quit function is in the next section. To end this program you'll need to use Ctrl+C.

6. Test the value that the user gives you. Use the strip method on selection: selection = selection.strip().

   This is a tiny bit of data cleaning. It removes blank spaces from the start and end of a string.

7. If selection isn't "1" or "2" or "3", (they're strings, remember?), then create a message asking the user to choose again.

   This process should loop until the user chooses one of those three options.

8. Create one function stub for do_quit().

   You already have two functions that you can use for these options: do_testing and display_times_tables for testing and training.

9. Create a docstring for it.

   Include a print statement identifying the function. It's useful for testing.

10. In the Main block, use an if/elif/else to call these functions based on the user's choice.

The Constants section has changed by adding this constant:

```
INSTRUCTIONS = """Welcome to Math Trainer
This application will train you on your times tables.
It can either print one or more of the tables for you
so that you can revise (training) or it can test
your times tables.
"""
```

This is the stub added to the Functions section:

```
def do_quit():
    """ quit the application"""
    print("In quit")
```

The Testing section is now entirely commented out. The following was added as a new Main section:

```
#### Main Section

if __name__ == "__main__":
    while True:
        print(INSTRUCTIONS)
        raw_input_prompt = "Press: 1 for training,"+\
                           " 2 for testing, 3 to quit.\n"
        selection = raw_input(raw_input_prompt)
```

```
    selection = selection.strip()
    while selection not in ["1", "2", "3"]:
        selection = raw_input("Please type either 1, 2 or 3: ")
        selection = selection.strip()

    if selection == "1":
        display_times_tables()
    elif selection == "2":
        do_testing()
    else:  # has to be 1, 2 or 3 so must be 3 (quit)
        do_quit()
```

Run through this four times to make sure things are working properly. Why four? Once to check that each of the three functions is called when the option is chosen and once to test the behavior when you make an invalid choice.

Add Quit Functionality

Now you need to get the quit feature working. Shouldn't be hard though, because you've dealt with that before in Project 5, where you improved your guessing game.

1. In the Imports section, add import sys.

   You'll use this for its sys.exit() function, which will cause the program to end.

2. Copy the confirm_quit() function that you covered in Project 5 into the Functions section.

3. Copy the constants that confirm_quit() relies on.

4. In the do_quit function, call confirm_quit().

   If the quit is confirmed, call sys.exit(). Otherwise, do nothing. The function will return and continue from where it was called.

This is the new `Imports` section:

```
#### Imports Section
import random
import sys
```

Awesome, huh? This constant had to be added to the `Constants` section. It came across from Project 5 with `confirm_quit`:

```
CONFIRM_QUIT_MESSAGE = 'Are you sure you want to quit (Y/n)? '
```

Just add this to the end of the constants that are already there.

I always have the urge to put constants in alphabetical order. I'm not sure that's a good idea. It's probably better to group constants by what they do. (For example, put LOWER and UPPER together because they're both used in the questioning functionality.)

The `confirm_quit` function was copied from Project 5:

```
def do_quit():
    """ quit the application"""
    if confirm_quit():
        sys.exit()
    print("In quit (not quitting, returning)")


def confirm_quit():
    """"Ask user to confirm that they want to quit
    default to yes
    Return True (yes, quit) or False (no, don't quit) """
    spam = raw_input(CONFIRM_QUIT_MESSAGE)
    if spam == 'n':
        return False
    else:
        return True
```

Keep the `print` statement in `do_quit` because it's useful for testing. (It only prints if you choose to quit, then change your mind.) The call to `sys.exit()` makes the application exit.

If you run the code from IDLE (like you do with all of the other code in the book), you might get a message like this:

```
Traceback (most recent call last):
  File "/data-current/dummies book/code folder/math_trainer_6.py",
            line 122, in <module>
    do_quit()
  File "/data-current/dummies book/code folder/math_trainer_6.py",
            line 68, in do_quit
    sys.exit()
SystemExit
```

It happens because of the way IDLE integrates running scripts while making the shell available. If you run this from outside IDLE, Python won't complain.

Polishing It Off

Tie up a couple of loose ends:

✔ Add a timing feature to the Testing section so you can report how much time the user took.

✔ Reset the maximum number of questions that will be asked in a round. Currently it's three.

✔ Tidy up and remove unused code.

It's downhill all the way from here.

Timing the questions

To time a round of questions, use the time module. Here's your 20-second introduction to it:

```
>>> import time
>>> time.time() # current time
1433075973.088198
```

Don't believe that's the current time? Check the docs: It's the current time in seconds since the Epoch. It's the exact time, down to one-millionth of a second, since January 1, 1970. Don't ask why. It's just another one of those historical accidents that infest everything that has to do with time calculations.

You can use the `time` module to get the difference in the times when two things happen, like this:

```
>>> t1 = time.time() # current time
>>> t2 = time.time()# current time again (I waited a smidge)
>>> t2-t1 # number of seconds between first and second calls
5.041269063949585
```

Have a look at `time.ctime` and `time.gmtime` sometime.

Now work on the timing stuff:

1. In the `Imports` section, import the `time` module

2. Set the `score` to 0 in the `do_testing` method, and get and store the current time in `start_time`:

   ```
   start_time = time.time()
   ```

3. Just before you print the score, grab the time again and store it in a separate variable. Figure the difference between these two variables.

4. Print the time taken, along with the score.

   Also print out what percentage of the questions was correct (score divided by total questions multiplied by 100). You can use the following as your template (add it to the `Constants` section). The doubled `%%` sign will print as a single `%`. The escape code `%.1f` says it's a floating point number with one decimal place:

   ```
   SCORE_TEMPLATE = "You scored %s (%i%%) in %.1f seconds"
   ```

The new `Imports` section looks like this:

```
#### Imports Section
import random
import sys
import time
```

There's a new constant in the `Constants` section:

```
SCORE_TEMPLATE = "You scored %s (%i%%) in %.1f seconds"
```

The reworked `do_testing` function looks like this now:

```
def do_testing():
    """ conduct a round of testing """
    question_list = make_question_list()
    score = 0
    start_time = time.time()
    for i, question in enumerate(question_list):
        if i >= MAX_QUESTIONS:
            break
        prompt = QUESTION_TEMPLATE%question
        correct_answer = question[0]*question[1]
            # indexes start from 0
        answer = raw_input(prompt)

        if int(answer) == correct_answer:
            print("Correct!")
            score = score+1
        else:
            print("Incorrect, should have been %s"%(correct_answer))

    end_time = time.time()
    time_taken = end_time-start_time
    percent_correct = int(score/float(MAX_QUESTIONS)*100)
    print(SCORE_TEMPLATE%(score, percent_correct, time_taken))
```

Tidying up the main application loop and the rest

Time to loop in the main application, the number of questions per test, and so on. You can do this! This stuff hardly even deserves its own section.

1. In the `Constants` section, amp up `MAX_QUESTIONS` to something like `10` or `20` (like `MAX_QUESTIONS = 10`).

   This will change the number of questions that will be asked in each round of `do_testing`. Don't make it too many, though.

2. Remove the `print` statements you included for debugging. Delete commented-out code.

The `print(INSTRUCTIONS)` code is within the loop. You could leave it out of the loop and add another option "4" to print the instructions again if you like.

Summary

While you were making your math trainer, you did this, too:

- Randomized a list using the `random.shuffle` function.

- Created a user interface that gives instructions, then allowed users to choose from different options.

- Added quit functionality and confirmed that users do actually want to quit (which, admittedly, you've done in the past).

- Used a `while` loop to slice up tables.

Index

About the Author

Brendan is the father of three, each of whom he loves dearly. He also loves Python — not so much as his kids — but enough to start a blog (`python4kids.brendanscott.com`) to teach his eldest how to code it. That was in 2010! One thing led to another and the site took off. Now he has the opportunity to spread his love of Python to many more kids. He really hopes this book helps you catch that spark that makes using Python so great.

Author's Acknowledgments

I'd like to thank the people at Wiley for asking me to write this book in the first place and for the work they put in to the technical and other editing.

Dedication

To my family.

Publisher's Acknowledgments

Executive Editor: Steven Hayes

Development Editor: Tonya Maddox Cupp

Technical Editor: Camille McCue

Sr. Editorial Assistant: Cherie Case

Project Coordinator: Antony Sami

Special Technical Help: Dexter Lim, Lewis Lim

Cover Image: © Wiley